FINANCIAL PLANNING BASICS

A Plain English Guide to Understanding the Components of a Solid Financial Plan

Jeffrey G. Marsocci, Esq.
Certified Medicaid Planner™
Accredited V.A. Attorney

Domestic Partner Publishing, LLC

For more information, go to www.CareAssistanceCenter.com

Note Regarding Information

As with any product, it is important to be clear about its intended purpose and use to avoid any misunderstandings. Specifically with writings about legal issues, it is noted that these materials are not a substitute for competent legal or financial counsel. The contents of this guide are instead written to provide information about common financial planning components and processes, and it is designed for general educational purposes only. The contents of this guide are not to be construed as legal or financial advice, and no attorney-client privilege and/or financial advisory or fiduciary relationship exists between the reader and the author and/or publisher. In addition, laws change frequently, and therefore you also are urged to speak with an attorney about changes in the law that may affect you.

Circular 230 Disclosure: To ensure compliance with requirements imposed by the Internal Revenue Service, unless specifically indicated otherwise, any tax advice contained in this communication (including any accompanying literature) was not intended or written to be used, and cannot be used, for the purpose of avoiding tax-related penalties or promoting, marketing, or recommending to another party any tax-related matter addressed herein. For specific legal advice, you are urged to contact an attorney in your state or jurisdiction.

About the Author

Jeffrey G. Marsocci was born in Fort Worth, Texas, and raised in Lincoln, Rhode Island, where he graduated from Mount Saint Charles Academy High School. He received his Bachelor's degree in Business from Hofstra University, and two years later earned his law degree from the same university.

In 2004, he received a Certificate Degree in Non-Profit Management from Duke University. Jeff also served as a member of the Legal Council for The Estate Planning Source, LLC, a nationally recognized estate preservation company formed by the protégés of the late Henry W. Abts III, trust guru and author of The Living Trust. In 2012, Mr. Marsocci was admitted as VA Accredited Attorney for the preparation, presentation, and prosecution of claims before the Department of Veterans Affairs in order to focus on assisting clients qualify for the Aid and Attendance Pension Benefit. In 2014, he was credentialed as a Certified Medicaid Planner™ by the CMP Governing Board for meeting education and experience requirements, showing proficiency in Medicaid Planning through a thorough examination, and committing to adhere to the highest in professional standards.

Mr. Marsocci has led his own firm in Raleigh, North Carolina, since 1996, focusing on the areas of VA Pension Benefit asset protection, Medicaid Planning, and general Trusts and Estate Planning. He also frequently participates in national and regional programs to educate attorneys, financial advisors and accountants on estate planning issues.

Jeff and his wife Kathleen work with the college-based service organization Circle K at North Carolina State University. Jeff and Kathy also each received the President's Call to Service Award for performing more than 4,000 hours of service during their lifetimes.

This book is dedicated to the rare financial advisors who help their clients see the whole picture instead of just the puzzle pieces they know and can help with.

Special Thanks to
Charles "Mike" Brooks
for his contributions to this book,
without whose help the book wouldn't be possible.

TABLE OF CONTENTS

Foreword

"The only source of knowledge is experience," said Albert Einstein. With over two decades of estate and trust planning, my colleague Jeffrey G. Marsocci has written an easy to understand guide to financial risk and wealth management.

Jeff spent many years working as an estate planning attorney. He told me the story of how he got into estate planning in the first place was because his grandfather passed on and didn't have an estate plan that avoided probate. The experience his grandmother had with probate while Jeff was in law school caused Jeff to focus on planning estates the right way to avoid these administrative problems if that was what the client wished. He focused on determining the goals the client wanted to achieve, and then find the right plan to help the clients reach their goals.

During his time as an estate planning attorney, Jeff not only worked with clients on their documents, but he also worked with them on making sure their financial accounts line up properly with their plan. With many of his clients having financial advisors, Jeff has seen that some clients have investments that financially lined up with their goals and stage of life, but some others did not. Jeff also has a background in assisting non-profits and businesses with strategic planning. And as I've gotten to know Jeff, one thing that truly sets him apart from most other attorneys is the ability to speak in plain English and get to the heart of the matter quickly.

All of these experiences and skills brought him to the realization that there are quite a few people out there who aren't determining what their true financial goals are before investing their hard earned money. And while there are many good financial advisors who look at all of the different investing options available, there are also some financial advisors who will only look at the different investing options that they specifically can provide. By applying the same process of determining goals and objectives that he uses in his law practice as well as in helping non-profit groups and clubs create strategic plans, Jeff has developed a process to find out a person's true financial goals and then structure a financial plan to help them meet their goals. Whether or not Jeff can personally help them with their finances.

But back to the estate planning part for a minute. It used to be estate planning was only important to the wealthy, but now more than ever even the middle class can benefit from an estate plan. (Especially since the estate tax is under heated debate and the government trying to close the deficit.) Estate planning revolves around net worth and future healthcare decisions. Net worth is made up all the assets you own including investments, cash accounts, retirement accounts, interests in businesses, life insurance, real estate, etc. With so much importance on your future, family, and legacy involving your financial wellbeing how necessary is it to have an experienced and knowledgeable estate attorney. The answer is very important and exactly why you should finish this book.

I've personally read several of Jeff's published books, and they are easy to understand, use plain English, educate and inform. After all, shouldn't we have an attorney with decades of experience planning estates using all of his client's net worth and financial assets give you a simple and informative guide towards ours?

I remember when the S&P broke 13,000 and crashed to under 8,000 in 2009. I was sitting in a client's kitchen reviewing his Medicare supplement insurance. He just turned 65 and I had placed him into a Medigap program to protect his net worth from medical expenses. We started discussing his retirement and I had planned on showing him a fixed indexed annuity to protect against market volatility and provide a guaranteed income. Simultaneously on the television the news was reporting a drastic drop in the markets. As I paused to listen, my client was already dialing his financial broker to move all his stocks into a money market account. Needless to say, he took a significant loss to his account, and, even though he moved fast, the markets move faster. At his age, was it prudent to have the majority of retirement sitting in the stock market? Considering his reaction to the news, I think both he and his wife wouldn't have taken such a significant loss if they truly had a plan that reflected their goals.

Having spent over a decade in the insurance industry, I've helped thousands of individuals and their families' protect their net worth with many of the safe type of money vehicles discussed in the next chapters. But I do understand that what I provide may only be one small piece of the puzzle for some, but a much larger piece for others. But we should be taking a look at each client's goals, tolerances for risk, and other factors in the process that Jeff outlines in this book. And, yes, finding out those goals and objectives also comes with some plain English education on the different types of investments available, which Jeff has also provided in this book.

Many of the same processes and principals I use in my business have been completely revamped since I've began working with Jeff because they just make sense for my clients. With heavy recruiting from insurance and brokerage companies for sales, many agents have less than even a year of experience when they make a financial planning recommendation for a potential client. Even I've made some not so great recommendations in the past simply from not having the knowledge that comes with understanding my client's goals and the nearly limitless options for financially meeting those goals. But now I've found that Jeff does have a process that can help get to the heart of the matter, and this book is the first step. It's clear that his twenty years of experience and knowledge from estate planning, financial planning, and even strategic planning has been poured into this book and into his office processes. If you value your own financial future, then this is a book you should finish to the end.

Mike Brooks
NC Licensed Insurance Advisor

Introduction

Several years ago, I was between estate planning seminars in Burlington with a financial advisor co-presenter I worked with, and he was meeting with a prospective client at the restaurant. I was asked to be in on the meeting just to review things and see if there was anything missing from a legal perspective, and I agreed. It was either helping out on the case or reviewing hundreds of pages of a new federal law that only tangentially affected my clients, so I was happy for an excuse to put the tome aside for a while. Plus it kept me from getting and eating more from the buffet.

"I really think you should take a look at the numbers," the financial advisor said. "The past two years have been flat, and the year before that you actually lost a good amount money, so you are actually down over the past three years. If this variable annuity is the main supplement to your social security, it has only gone down and is not helping you reach your retirement goals."

The man looked skeptical, but the numbers weren't lying. He had lost money since he put money into the account, and he realized it, but just kept rubbing his beard as if he were thinking. But I didn't say anything yet because I was still looking over his annuity statements and his tax returns, trying to get the full picture.

"But the advisor has been helping my brother out for years now, and he sold me this annuity," he said. "My brother plays golf with him and swears by him. I don't know if it's time to move since I've already put three years into this annuity, and I'm still two years from retirement at age 67. I'm wondering if I should just keep it the way it is for now."

"But has your investment done what you wanted it to do?" the advisor asked.

That was when I saw two very interesting numbers and actually did a double take. I was starting to see just how bad the variable annuity had been to him.

"Excuse me, I don't really want to interrupt," I said. "But I just want to make sure these numbers are correct."

Both the client and the financial advisor stopped and looked at me with rapt attention.

"Looking at last year's tax returns, it says you paid almost $7,500 in federal taxes," I said. "Is that correct?"

"Yes," he replied. "So?"

"And your annuity statement shows that you paid a little more than $7,800 in fees," I said. "Is that correct?"

He just looked at me with a blank stare.

"According to these statements, you actually paid your golf-playing broker more money than you paid to Uncle Sam, and the broker lost you money." I said. "Are you sure you just want to let it ride?"

There are always different kinds of investments with a lot of information, misinformation, and confusion out there. Things are almost never as simple as they could be, and I've seen my clients get caught up in bad, or at least inappropriate, investments for them and their goals. And their financial advisor is not always doing the best thing for the client.

One reason is the common but mistaken belief that you will have one set of goals and investment criteria, and it will always be that way. That is simply not true. In fact, in many cases people's investment parameters will change greatly with age and health needs. Simply staying the course for 30 or 40 years is not going to reflect changed life circumstances and will not serve you well in the long run.

So why am I going into this? I've been an estate planning and Medicaid planning attorney for a few decades now, so why talk about investing? It's because I've seen far too many of my clients get burned by bad investments at the hands of salespeople using the title of financial advisor. They had a product they wanted to sell that made them more money, and it didn't matter what was actually best for them.

There have also been smear campaigns against certain investments being lumped together when the type of investments couldn't be more different. I'm mainly talking about annuities. It's gotten so bad that what could be highly effective investment vehicles for a particular client's situation is not even being looked at because of the systematic, engineered discrediting of *all* annuities when the ones with problems are mainly *variable* annuities being misused.

Variable annuities are just investments placed in the stock market but wrapped in a contract that allows a person to convert it into an income stream. There is typically no guaranteed growth of the underlying assets, and what has deservedly earned variable annuities a bad reputation is that there are often high management fees associated with it. So the broker and their company make a lot of money no matter what, and the client may end up watching their investments go down a lot more than if they just kept their money in the market because they are being "fee'd" to death.

So why aren't variable annuities just outlawed? Because they actually do serve a good purpose for the right clients. When clients have 10 or more years until retirement and they are intentionally planning to turn the variable annuity into an income stream at retirement, then it might be a very appropriate place to invest. After all, who really cares about the fees or how far the market falls if the goal is to turn it into an income stream no matter what? It's only if the income amount falls based on the market that you have to be worried about things. But in general variable annuities are not for seniors looking to grow their money without a deliberate intention to turn on the income stream at a pre-determined time.

The kind of annuities that may be a lot more appropriate for seniors are those guaranteed not to lose the principal investment. And there are a lot of different kinds of these annuities with lots of different included or add-on features depending on the individual annuity contracts and companies. In many cases, even the most risk-averse senior will want to have a mix of different assets, only one of which may be a guaranteed annuity.

But it's not just annuities versus stocks. It's financial professionals often not taking a look at changes over the long term and in a *comprehensive* manner; meaning looking at all investment options periodically and not just going from aggressive stocks to moderate stocks at some point. The purpose of this book is to give you a very broad overview of the different kinds of investments out there, what they do and do not do, and how to approach figuring out what is right for you at this stage of life. It will provide you with a way to looking more broadly at your investments and what you want them to do for you. No one investment is right for everybody at every stage of their life and in every situation. You and your money deserve a better, systematic approach to taking hold of your financial future.

So sit down, grab a pen and notepad, and enjoy. A more secure financial future awaits.

Chapter One: The Stock Market

I was sitting in my father's study, which really wasn't used by him as a study. As a surgeon, my father had plenty of desk space at his actual office downtown, but the room was there with a desk and bookshelves. But my sister and I mainly used that room to watch TV away from the family room if my father was watching golf or basketball.

It was a Monday night in October of my senior year of high school, and as I was pushing buttons on the "pre-remote" television set to change the channel, I stopped at the national evening news to hear about the stock market crashing. As I watched and listened, I started to get worried. I know that all of the money being put aside for college was in the stock market, and I started to wonder if I would be able to afford it if the market really was as bad as they were saying. About twenty-three percent of the market was lost in a single day. October 19, 1987. Black Monday. Almost twenty-three percent lost. In one day.

And I had just sent out my college applications and was starting to think about visiting campuses in the Spring. Would I still be able to go? Would I have to work for a few years before college? Should I think about military service and the G.I. bill? Would I have to get some student loans? I had no idea. I decided to talk to my father about it.

"Don't worry about it," my father told me. "College will be paid for just as my parents paid for my college. Your job is to keep your grades up and get into a good college."

That was all well and good, but he did look a little worried.

As I remember that day when thinking about my clients, I have to wonder if I felt like that when I was 17 years old with my whole life ahead of me, how would my clients who are already retired feel about losing almost a quarter of their life savings in one day? They'd probably look a lot worse than my father did that day.

The stock market is your chance to have your money make money. You invest in various companies through stocks, and over time the value (and your investment) grows. The value of your stocks rises as the stock market rises, provided you have invested in the right companies. These corporations provide products and services to the public, and the better they are at doing that, the higher the demand for the stock is. When you place your bet on a corporation by buying its stock and the company grows, then you, my friend, are riding high.

Or the company can crash and burn, and you lose most or even all of your money.

Investing in the stock market is an incredible opportunity to put your money to work. But there is definitely risk involved. By buying stocks, you're giving your money to the corporation and telling it to go to work. Or you're buying the stock from someone who previously put their money in it, and you're giving them your money to take over their ownership interest. But since there are no 100% accurate crystal balls, no one can predict the future and tell you with certainty that your company will succeed. They could grow enormously, or they could tank, or something in between.

It's also not just the company that may succeed or fail, but an entire industry could rise or fall. The Dot Com bubble burst in 2000 with Internet development companies previously growing exponentially each year only for it to come crashing down as the business world realized that the Internet was important but not THAT important. Private security firms, construction groups, and supply companies all specializing in war zone deployment were very profitable in the early to middle 2000s, but they then saw their work cut dramatically as the Iraq and Afghanistan occupations receded. In general, those industries fell, and it greatly impacted their stock prices. The better companies retooled and did something else or found other markets, but not all of them survived. And the stock values adjusted accordingly.

Even more broadly speaking, entire indices can change, not just certain sectors of the market. Take the Nikkei, for example. The Nikkei is a Japanese investment stock index that bought and utilized hard assets, such as real estate and artwork. In February of 1985, the Nikkei Index was at a high of 260.34. Over the next five years, the Nikkei dropped to 129.01 in November of 1990. That's correct… it lost half of its value in five years.

"But wait a minute," I keep hearing "the market always comes back. Doesn't it?"

Usually it does. But not necessarily on *your* timetable. Here are some portfolio returns for ten years of investing based on the S&P 500 index using $500,000 to invest. But we change the start year in these three examples.* (Calculations made using https://dqydj.com/sp-500-return-calculator/ and not adjusted for inflation.)

January 1996 to January 2006

Initial Investment: $500,000

Percentage Return: 108.12%

Portfolio End Value: $1,040,600.00

January 2001 to January 2011

Initial Investment: $500,000

Percentage Return: -3.969%

Portfolio End Value: $480,155.00

January 2006 to January 2016

Initial Investment: $500,000

Percentage Return: 50.039%

Portfolio End Value: $750,195

Do you have time for your investments to come back? If you were ready to retire in 2002 and planned on using some of your investments, you probably had to either severely downgrade your standard of living or keep working. And a lot of people did keep working. Same thing with people retiring in 2007. Although the market did come back from the crash in 2008-2009, it would have been extremely rough going having your savings crash just when you needed to start taking money out. And that means that the more than 50% return over ten years would be much less since you were drawing money out for your retirement. On the other hand, here's what $500,000 invested in the market in 1996 and not needed until 2016 (20 years) looks like:

<u>January 1996 to January 2016</u>

Initial Investment:	$500,000
Percentage Return:	212.262%
Portfolio End Value:	$1,561,310.00

Your money more than tripled over a twenty year period in the S&P 500! Which is fantastic, but you had twenty years for your investments to grow. Yes, the stock market is often the highest potential for gain. On the other hand, it also has the potential for losses if you don't have enough time for the market to recover. Unless you have that more than 20 years before retirement, you might want to consider other investment options.

Chapter Two:
Investing Through the Years

I was genuinely concerned about the Henderson's financial picture. It was March of 2008, which meant they had been estate planning clients for more than ten years. But now that Tom was turning 65 and thinking of retiring, we took a harder look at the Henderson's finances in addition to their estate planning wishes. Back then, I was not in a position to actually help with finances, but I knew enough to have the clients discuss my concerns with their financial advisor.

"These brokerage accounts have been treating us well for a good number of years now," Tom said. "I don't see why we should change things up."

"Because you are thinking of retirement," I said. "What you have now is enough to meet and even exceed your projected needs. But if the market falls, who knows if it will still be enough?"

"But we rode through the tech bubble bursting in 2000," Glenda said. "The market always comes back. At least that's what our broker tells us."

"It's true," I said. "The market always does come back. But sometimes is takes quite a few years for it to come back. With Tom retiring in a year or two and then you retiring a year or two after that, do you have enough time for the market to come back before you start taking money out? You can't keep investing like you are 30 or even 40 anymore. As my clients get older, they tend to preserve the principal for more of the assets they have grown while lowering the amount of assets that are at risk in the market that could rise or fall with the economy."

Tom and Glenda looked at each other and frowned. "Well, we'll have to talk to our broker about that," Tom said dismissively, and that was that.

It wasn't a year, or two years, but three years later when Tom and Glenda came back in to talk about some estate planning changes as well as their finances. They were happy to see that the market was starting to come back from their portfolio's 22% loss in 2008-2009, but they still hadn't come close to recovering what they lost. Tom and Glenda were both still working well past the ages they planned on, and probably would be for a few years yet. They just couldn't afford to stop working right now because they had to put back what the market lost.

What makes sense for you at 30 doesn't make sense for you at 40, or 50, or 60, or 70. You could end up losing money that you can't afford to lose. And investing like you are 70 when you are 30 also doesn't make sense because you can miss out on so many opportunities. Unfortunately, the world is replete with financial advisors and stock brokers who have the same exact products for all ages, with only certain tweaks to account for your age and risk tolerance. In other words, they are the hammer that sees all investing as nails, and they miss using the right tools out of the toolbox for the best overall results for their clients.

We see it all the time when clients are in their 60s and 70s. They have been investing with the same brokerage firm for many, many years, and they have ridden the ups and downs. In all, they have probably grown their assets considerably, but then a crash hits the market, and suddenly they've lost 25% of their portfolio. In early 2017, one of my clients complained that her brokerage account hit a peak in 1998, but then the highs and lows under her advisor's direction now had her account value at half its 1998 value. That is not good news for someone in her late 60s.

I also had the fortune to speak with much younger investor in his late 30s who wanted to grow his money, but his family experienced so many losses with stock investing at the wrong time that he was completely unwilling to put money in anything other than banks CDs, treasury bonds, and savings accounts that were FDIC insured. "I intend to work for my money, not for my money to work for me," he said. "My family has always said that smart people have money work for them and not the other way around. But those family members always tend to be broke."

I tried to explain the concept of balancing investments across different age groups, but it took a long time before I could assure him that it is OK to have some money in the market at his age. We just want to make sure that we had a gradual, planned shift away from risk-based investments the older he got. Now he is on the right track to letting at least a portion of his money take market risk because he has 25 years before he is even coming close to retiring.

But what is the right mixture of investments for you? Where do people like you fit in to the investment spectrum? Just as it is a disservice to tell someone they should always be investing in stocks because the person giving the advice is a stock broker, I would be doing you a disservice if I told you that you should be investing a certain way based solely on your age. However, here is where I see *a lot of people* in certain age brackets *leaning* with their portfolio, but it is by no means definitive. The only way to be sure what works for you is to go through a comprehensive Financial Strategy Session

Ages 25-40

The best age to put money away and invest more aggressively in stocks tends to be when you are younger and have a lot of time for falls in the market to come back. A twenty-five percent loss in the market is tough, but when you still have 25-40 years, the market has consistently rebounded and had more than enough good years to offset the bad. While certain rainy day funds and regular bank accounts need to be kept in safety, money in 401ks and mutual funds can be more aggressive. In simple terms, for money you won't need or depend on for a few decades, there is no reason not to be more aggressive. At some point around age 40, preferably when the market is on a high note, it will be time to think about transferring a percentage of money from stocks into safer investments, or at the least move some stocks from aggressive to conservative.

Ages 41-55

While early forties to mid-fifties is a time usually marked by higher earnings, it also may be a time for higher expenses, especially if kids are being put through college. But it is still important to save for retirement, and more and more of our clients want to start toning down the aggressiveness of their investing strategies. It's not just about going from aggressive to moderate stock investments; it's actually making sure that some portion is guaranteed safe, even if it is only 25% of what you are investing. While many of our clients look at bank CDs and money market accounts for safety, they are often disappointed in the returns they get. So for the amount that they do want kept guaranteed safe and not to lose money, there are life insurance and annuities that are not directly invested in the stock market that can provide much better returns on average. The remainder of the investments are often kept in stocks because there is still time for the market to come back, but the now-lowered percentage that is still invested in the market often shifts from aggressive to moderate.

Ages 56-65

The decade before the traditional age of retirement is now marked by much more careful investing, and there is a much larger focus on preserving what has been saved over risking what you have in the market in the hopes of bigger gains. This is also when discussions invariably turn to thoughts of having sufficient income in retirement, but too often people look to their stocks to see what dividends are being paid out rather than looking at other financial arrangements to eventually convert them into streams of income in retirement. In this age group, many are looking at a maximum of 25% being invested in the stock market, and even that percentage is most likely in moderate to conservative investments. The remaining 75% is in often different guaranteed, secure investments like bank CDs, real estate, and a good amount in fixed and indexed annuities.

Age 65+

The golden years of retirement are marked with extremely conservative investing, often with 100% in safe and secured investments such as bank CDs, fixed and indexed annuities, and stock, if there is any, is in very conservative and long-standing companies. Even real estate that might have been kept as rental properties tend to be sold off just as soon as the market is good enough and the proceeds reinvested in secure and guaranteed investments. For many of my clients, this is not a time to lay awake worrying that the latest market crash means that they can't afford to fly out to visit the grandchildren. At this stage, my clients who are still heavily invested in the stock market will begin to move their money into annuities and other guaranteed safe vehicles, or, unfortunately, they end up suffering a crash and only then move what's left into guaranteed safe investments.

For everything under the sun there is a season. And this is just as true with investing. When the years of taking risks start to go by, our smart clients will start to shift their assets to preserve what gains they've made. But just because they are looking at guaranteed safe investments doesn't mean that they have to settle for bank CD rates that might not even keep up with inflation. And, conversely, just because someone is still really young doesn't mean they should be OK putting everything in high risk stocks. There are a lot of different types of investments with varying degrees of risk, and we want to give you an overview of the main types out there.

Chapter Three: Different Investment Types

I was very saddened to hear of Charlie Ross suddenly passing on. It was always a joy meeting with him and his wife Cecelia, or "Sissy" for short. Thankfully, we had planned well for their estates with the proper revocable living trust and other documents. But now Sissy was out of her depth in managing her own finances.

Charlie was one of those rare people who actually knew more than his broker did, and he put in the time to really understand what he was doing. Charlie and Sissy were retired, so Charlie spent a lot of his time scouring the internet for information on companies he was thinking of investing in, and Sissy sat right beside him with a small TV and her crocheting. Despite being right there with him, Sissy had no interest in investing, and she didn't have to; she could just leave it all to Charlie. She certainly didn't want to do thirty hours of research a week just to pick the right stocks or funds, which is what Charlie did.

Sissy just didn't know where to start. "I have no idea what to do," Sissy told me. "I ran the household budget, but I never really knew where the money was coming from when we needed things. I handled the bills, the budget, and the grocery shopping, but Charlie's job was making sure we had enough money to meet our needs."

While they were both in their late 60s when Charlie passed on, Charlie had placed their finances largely in brokerage accounts with a decent "rainy day fund" in a money market account. That plus their small house, vacation townhouse, and the limited bank accounts for monthly income and expenses rounded out more than $2 million of net worth. But the greatest percentage of assets was in the brokerage account under Charlie's direct control.

But there was now a pretty big hole in their overall financial plan because Charlie's pension was gone. "First thing's first," I told Sissy. "Let's take a look at your guaranteed income plus regular expenses. From there, we can take a look at what we need to do with your investments. The investments are actually secondary to making sure that you have what you need coming in each month."

After spending some time going over the changed income versus adjusting bills for one person instead of two, the loss in income could easily be made up. "Based on your reduced needs, it really wouldn't be too much to make up the income you need," I told Sissy, a look of relief washing over her face. "We can either plan to draw down assets slowly over time to make up the shortfall, or look at an immediate annuity. We should take a look at both options, but in order to make that decision, we really should look at how you want to handle the investments."

She suddenly looked very anxious. "I have no idea where to start," she said.

"Let's start at the beginning with the basics," I said, smiling. "We need to know what tools are out there and what they do before we decide where we want things to go."

Investments are as diverse as the number of birds in the sky and the number of fish in the ocean. There are all kinds of places to invest money to grow, all kinds of permutations of those investments, and then all manner of features on top of the permutations of the investments. But let's step back for a second and take a look at five very specific *categories* of investments. This chapter will look at these general categories and then subsequent chapters will dig a little deeper into the different *kinds* of investments in each category.

Bank Accounts and CDs

Probably the most frequent investments for anyone are the traditional bank instruments. Since I was 14, I have always had checking and savings accounts, even if they initially had to be cosigned by a parent. But going back even further, when my mother took me and my sister on errands, we would often end up at the bank, and we carefully examined all of the different brochures and deposit slips at the counter, even before we could read. Growing up for most of us, we learned that the bank is where you kept your money.

And that is good and necessary for the usual cash flow of paychecks coming in and bills being paid going out. But as people progress and build assets beyond living paycheck to paycheck, banks often had other options for savings money and earning more money. Bank CDs, money market accounts, and even treasury bills come under this category.

The common characteristics of these types of investments are usually little or even no interest, *but* they are government backed and secure. The Federal Deposit Insurance Corporation, more commonly known as (FDIC), is a government corporation created by the Glass-Steagall Act of 1933 that currently provides deposit insurance of a certain amount. Currently this means that deposits by a person held in member banks are insured up to $250,000 per depositor per bank.

While this deposit insurance is extremely helpful in keeping banks safe and stable by boosting confidence, many people mistakenly believe that ALL funds in a bank are insured, and they aren't. In addition, many people feel that in recent years the security of a bank being FDIC insured is not enough to justify the limited returns that people get.

Real Estate

As complicated as things are with securities, as you will see below, things become even more *personally* complicated when real estate is involved. Most people who purchase real estate do so for their own use. They buy a home and live in it. They purchase a vacation home, and they use it on vacation. They buy into a timeshare and use it their one or two weeks out of the year. In these cases, there is often little initial thought given to how real estate values rise or fall. On the whole, the value of real estate often grows over time, sometimes even more than the stock market. But the value of their real estate is irrelevant to them until the time comes to sell it. After all, what difference does it really make if the real estate market crashes and your home loses 50% of its value if the reason you have it is to live in it?

Other clients of ours actually look at real estate as an investment, and they manage it accordingly. However, it does take a lot of time and effort, particularly if you are the property manager of your own rental properties. When a call comes in because a water heater burst, you have to go and fix or replace it. When a toilet clogs, you have to go fix it. And when a termite inspection shows bad news, you have to bear the cost of extermination and repairs. But having the income from rental properties can be a great boon. Unless, of course, you end up with several units vacant at any given time.

And if you are simply buying, renovating, and selling properties, if the market falls, you are out of a lot of cash if you hold the property, or you may lose on a deal if you need cash and have to sell low. In all cases, directly owning real estate means that your money is extremely illiquid. You may be able to make a lot of money in real estate, but if you can't sell or rent properties but need cash, you may be out of luck. For many of our clients, there comes a time when being a landlord or playing the real estate "flipping" game is not for them anymore.

Stocks, Bonds, and Mutual Funds

The second most common category used as an investment behind bank accounts are market securities, or "stocks, bonds, and mutual funds." These are investments that have a huge potential to grow money, but at the same time these investments have a huge potential to lose money. There is no guarantee around the loss of money in most of these instruments, and great care should be used when investing in securities, especially if they are not part of a broadly-based compilation of stocks like a mutual fund. Economic conditions rise, and generally stocks will rise. But even if the economic conditions rise in many areas but fall in the one main area your stocks are invested in, your portfolio will still drop.

When it comes to the stock market, it is always good to keep in mind the mathematical structure of gains and losses. For example, if you start the year with $500,000 in the stock market and it falls 25% in that one year, then you have $375,000 of stocks left. If in the next year the market rises 25%, then your stocks are only at $468,750. With the same fall and then rise of 25%, your stocks still aren't back to where they started. But what if it happens the other way around? Your stocks start at $500,000 and gain 25% to reach a value of $625,000 in one year. Then the next year the market and your stocks lose 25% of its value, and now your $625,000 becomes... $468,750. You still aren't ahead no matter whether the rise or fall happens first. It is only by much bigger gains than losses over time that your money will grow.

Gold, Art, and Other Fixed Assets

This is the catch-all, "miscellaneous" category of assets that many people might have only an item or two in, but not very often are they really considered an investment by the people who hold them. However, we would be remiss to not mention these investments because some people certainly do have them, and in some cases they might have some significant value.

Probably the most common of the miscellaneous assets are gold and other precious metals, whether in rare coins or simply as weighed metal. (For this category specifically, we're not talking about gold or silver "funds," but actually having the metal on hand or in a safe deposit box.) We have had clients with one or two rare paintings worth about $100,000 collectively, but it was by no means among the vast collections that some people have.

Still others have some antiques of significant value. One of our client's mothers had an antique furniture business, so in addition to her business inventory of about $200,000 in antiques at her death, there was also about $300,000 worth of antique furniture she personally collected and kept in her house. And I don't think anyone would dispute that half a million dollars in antiques is not worthy of mentioning.

With the exception of precious metals, this category of investments is often characterized as being hard to value and not usually easy to liquidate, at least not at a fair price. It by no means is as illiquid as real estate because those are big transactions, but it is illiquid just because there may be a much more limited pool of potential buyers willing to pay what the assets are worth. Except for our most wealthy clients, we don't usually see people in retirement wanting to buy and sell antiques and artwork on a regular basis. They'll either divest those assets over time, or they intend for them to be passed down as family heirlooms.

Life Insurance and Annuities

More than any of the other asset categories, life insurance and annuities are extraordinarily varied in form and function, and therefore are the most misunderstood. People try to find common threads among *all* life insurance and *all* annuities in an attempt to figure out what *every* life insurance policy or annuity must be and do, and it is just not that simple.

For life insurance, the common factor is that when the insured person dies, a death benefit pays out. Every life insurance policy has an owner, a person who is insured, and a beneficiary or beneficiaries that get paid a death benefit. That's it. That's where the commonalities end and the different features and options can go off into wildly different directions, but that really just means that there are more options to choose from in selecting the right policy (or even policies) that suit particular needs and overall financial plan. And even upon death, the beneficiary can often actually choose among a variety of payout options, so even then it is not accurate to just say that the beneficiary *must* just get a big check for their whole amount.

Annuities are just as varied. *However, annuities are also classified as life insurance.* Every annuity has an owner, a person who is insured, and a beneficiary or beneficiaries that get paid a death benefit. Same as life insurance. One difference, though, is that annuities always have some option to convert the assets in the account into a stream of income. The income may be paid monthly, quarterly, annually, or by some other arrangement. It may pay out for the rest of your life, or over a 6 month period, or some other set time frame. It just depends on the different options in the particular annuity.

While the commonalities for all life insurance and all annuities are pretty basic, there are great differences among many types of annuities and life insurance policies as well as features the particular companies creates in them. Therefore, there are also many other potential uses for life insurance and annuities that go well beyond paying a death benefit when someone dies or being able to trigger a stream of income. There are reasons that life insurance and annuities are quickly becoming the investment tools of today and the future, and that is why we are devoting a whole chapter to it in this book.

A Note About Retirement Accounts

We would be remiss if we didn't talk about retirement accounts, such as IRAs, 401ks, 403bs and others. But it also isn't entirely accurate to say that they are really a separate category of *investment.* The fact is that just about every type of asset we discussed can make up a retirement account, but the real distinction is how the account is taxed. Whether it is stocks or mutual funds, or annuities, or even commercial real estate inside an IRA, what is important is that the investment grows without any income or capital gains taxes being due each year, there are tax deductions for contributing to these accounts, but when money comes out it is taxed. It is also subject to minimum amounts being required to come out at certain ages, and because the accounts are for retirement if you take money out too early you also pay a penalty.

For many of our clients, their two biggest investments are their home and their retirement accounts, however the investments inside the retirement accounts are made up, so we have devoted an entire chapter to explaining these tax-deferred retirement accounts versus non-deferred accounts.

As you can see, there are many different categories of assets, but this chapter is just an overview. Each category has its own chapter in this book. But because the taxation of these accounts matters quite a bit when thinking about investments in general, we'll start next with a chapter on tax-deferral.

Chapter Four:
Tax-Deferred and Non-Deferred

Sixty-five year old Don Michaels sat across from me, looking at the numbers I was proposing. He scrunched up his face making his reading glasses move. And then he started shaking his head while talking. "So, you're saying I should actually take money out of my IRA next year?" Don said. "But that means I'll pay more in taxes! No way!"

"But if you don't, you're going to turn 70½ and up having to take out a lot more money each year later on," I said. "Then you'll really be bumping against much higher rates. According to the calculations we've put together, keeping your IRA compounding without withdrawals means that you will have a high pension, social security, and then much bigger withdrawals in six years at the higher tax rates. If you live to life expectancy, you'll end up paying close to $90,000 more in taxes by waiting."

"No, paying taxes is always bad," he said. "I don't want to pay any more in taxes than I have to."

"Then I'm not sure if you want to see another possible strategy," I said. "We can actually make your overall tax position better by converting some IRA assets into Roth IRAs over the next two years."

"What do you mean?" he asked, scrunching his face again.

"We can actually withdraw even more money to pay the taxes, and then put the funds into a Roth IRA," I said. "Then the money in the Roth IRA can actually grow tax free. That could net you about $250,000 in income tax savings."

Don started to look positively when I said tax free. "So what does that mean for my income taxes?"

"It does mean paying more taxes in the next two years so…"

"No, no, no," Don said. "I'm not going to pay any more taxes than I have to."

"Then you'll probably end up igniting a tax bomb later on," I said. "To the tune of a quarter of a million dollars more than you have to."

Don's situation is not unique. There are always taxes to pay when you make money, but the government will often structure taxes not just to raise revenue, but to give tax breaks to encourage what it deems "good behavior." The government has health savings accounts to put money away with a tax deduction, and no income taxes will be paid on the stashed away money provided it is spent on health care. This can come in handy if there are large deductibles and co-pays required under health insurance.

Giving people an income tax break to put money away for retirement, up to a point, also makes sense to the government. After all, the government doesn't want people to end up broke or being 100% dependent on social security during retirement; they want seniors to also support spending into the economy during retirement. Our country has been through periods of mass poverty for seniors unable to work, and we don't want to go back to a time when if you couldn't work then you were left to die. Social Security ensures that seniors won't die from lack of basic necessities provided they worked and paid into the system. Allowing money to grow tax-deferred in retirement accounts incentivizes people to pay for a greater level their own support and a better lifestyle during retirement.

At the same time, the government doesn't want people to stash away that money without paying taxes on it and NOT having it eventually flow into the economy during retirement. This is why there are "required minimum distributions," sometimes called "required mandatory distributions" or simply "RMDs." We'll talk about RMDs in a moment.

So how exactly do these accounts work? The theory is pretty simple, and there are different types of accounts that have, over time, emerged to really not be that different from each other. So generally the steps are:

- Before retirement, put money away each year (up to a certain limit), and then you can deduct what you put away from your income taxes. In other words, you are putting aside "pre-tax" dollars for retirement.

- The money is invested in a variety of ways depending on your investment risk tolerance, and the investments can be, with a few exceptions, exactly what you can legally invest in outside of a retirement account.

- The money grows and grows (hopefully), but you do not pay any taxes on dividends, interest, or capital gains each year as you do with other types of investments.

- You cannot take the money out of your account until you reach 59½ years of age without both paying income taxes on the withdrawal AND a ten percent (10%) penalty.

- When you reach 59½, you can withdraw money without the ten percent penalty, but every dollar you withdraw is taxed as income that year.

- When you reach 70½, the government REQUIRES a minimum amount come out of the account and be taxed, and this is computed using IRS tables based on life expectancy.

These are the RMDs mentioned earlier. While we always tell our clients to have an accountant review their specific situation and give exact numbers, the general way to think about these withdrawals are that if you are 70½ and the IRS tables say you are supposed to die at 95½, then you have 25 years of life left. So that year you have to take out one twenty-fifth, or 4%. The next year, you have 24 years left, so you have to take out one twenty-fourth, or about 4.167%, and the next year it is one twenty-third, or 4.348%, etc. And if you "beat the tables" and actually live longer than the IRS tables said you should have, then you basically take out half each year until the account is closed.

You can always take out more than your RMD each year, but it is taxed as income. But this is not something that you need fear, like Mr. Michaels does. It just should be planned to make sure that *overall* you are not paying more in taxes than you need to, regardless of the tax situation in any one given year.

Now, what kind of tax-deferred retirement accounts are out there? We'll go over the big ones.

IRAs

IRAs are "Individual Retirement Arrangements" and are commonly miscalled "Individual Retirement Accounts." Basically, this is a private retirement account arrangement where a person can, within limits, put away money for retirement. Just as described above, you put pre-tax money into an IRA, it grows without taxes on dividends, interest, or capital gains. One of the best features of an IRA over 401k or 403b is that legally *you* determine the type of investments, not anyone else.

401ks

Classified by the section numbering in the tax code, 401ks are tax-deferred retirement accounts for employees of for-profit organizations. In some cases, companies have an employment incentive to put money into a 401k by matching the employee's contributions up to a certain percentage or dollar amount. The rules are generally the same as IRAs except technically the employer determines the investments within the 401k. Because employers can control the investments, many retiring employees will simply "roll over" their 401k into an IRA because their employer isn't matching any more contributions.

However, in a practical sense, the fact that an employer can manage the investments in a 401k has become largely moot. Many people remember the Enron debacle of the early 2000s and the fallout. One of the worst results of the fraud and deception was that their employees' 401ks were heavily invested in Enron stock. When the stock crashed, the employees had their retirement funds similarly crash, some losing 90% of their value.

Since the Enron crash, and even before that, many companies wanted to divest themselves from having to run their employees' 401ks… and the possibility they would be blamed for market losses by their employees because they would have invested things differently. That is why 401k management is often completely outsourced to financial investment firms with the employees themselves calling the shots. As a result, most employers have essentially limited their involvement to paying in any matching funds to the financial firm and nothing more.

403bs

While for-profit organizations have their own retirement code section, the 403b account is for non-profits and public sector retirement. Many of our clients who are teachers or retired teachers may have 403bs in addition to or in place of a regular pension. The rules are generally the same as 401ks, but previously the scope of investments was more limited. Different changes over time have now limited the differences between 401ks and 403bs to mainly vesting periods when employees are entitled to get a 403b opened.

As you can see, there really aren't too many differences anymore between IRAs, 401ks, 403bs, and other tax-deferred retirement accounts. At least not many that matter to the average person. For that reason, we won't waste time going into the different eccentricities of these types of accounts, and we may just refer to them as retirement accounts or even just IRAs in the remainder of the book.

Non-Deferred Accounts

With a few exceptions noted below, if an account is not tax-deferred, then it is a "non-deferred" account. This means that if investments kick out income, such as dividends for stocks, then you will end up paying income taxes on that income. If you have assets being bought and then sold for more money, such as stocks, then there are capital gains taxes associated with that sale. So each year, there are capital gains taxes reported. (There are some exemptions and deductions and ways to defer capital gains, but for now, let's leave any specific questions on that to the accountants.)

In short, if your investment pays out income, then you pay income taxes. If you sell an asset for a higher price than you purchased it, then you have capital gains taxes to deal with. On the one hand, you lose out on some compounding of value since, presumably, you have to take money from somewhere in order to pay the taxes each year. On the other hand, if you end up liquidating a sizeable portion of non-deferred investments, it is not as if the whole amount you draw out is considered taxable income. After all, you've been paying taxes on the income all along.

And now, we have a few exceptions because there are some investments that are not wholly in either the tax-deferred or non-deferred camp that deserve special attention…

Tax Deferral of Non-Retirement Accounts

While this chapter is mainly on tax deferred accounts for retirement, there are also ways to shelter investments from paying income and capital gains taxes on investments year to year *even with investments that are not tax-deferred.* I often tell my clients that if they think the oil and gas lobbies have tremendous power to influence legislation in Congress, that's nothing compared to the insurance industry. So there are some very clever loopholes in the tax code that allows growth of investments inside certain life insurance products to be tax-deferred until the money is distributed.

For example, if someone has $500,000, and they want to invest it in a fund that mirrors the S&P 500, then the fund would have dividends and capital gains taxes payable each year. However, the same $500,000 investment inside an annuity contract, which is technically a type of life insurance, could defer the income and capital gains taxes until money is withdrawn years later. This could make for some clever tax planning indeed.

While that $500,000 going in is not technically what most advisors would call "tax-deferred," the gains and growth are. It's just that the $500,000 going in is after-tax dollars.

Roth IRAs

One of the more recent types of accounts (at least compared to 401ks and IRAs) are Roth IRAs, and there are some big tax considerations around these accounts that could save you massive amounts of money in the long run.

Basically, Roth IRAs allow you to pay the taxes on retirement money ahead of time so that the growth happens tax free AND the withdrawals are also tax free. For example, if you are under 50, you can contribute up to $5,500 in 2017, but with certain limits depending on your income. Once you are over 50, that contribution jumps to $6,500. If a 30 year old contributes $5,500 each year for 20 years and it grows at 6%, the value will look like this:

Year	Contribution	Growth Rate	Balance
2017	$5,500	0.06	$ 5,830.00
2018	$5,500	0.06	$ 12,009.80
2019	$5,500	0.06	$ 18,560.39
2020	$5,500	0.06	$ 25,504.01
2021	$5,500	0.06	$ 32,864.25
2022	$5,500	0.06	$ 40,666.11
2023	$5,500	0.06	$ 48,936.07
2024	$5,500	0.06	$ 57,702.24
2025	$5,500	0.06	$ 66,994.37
2026	$5,500	0.06	$ 76,844.03
2027	$5,500	0.06	$ 87,284.68
2028	$5,500	0.06	$ 98,351.76
2029	$5,500	0.06	$ 110,082.86
2030	$5,500	0.06	$ 122,517.83
2031	$5,500	0.06	$ 135,698.90
2032	$5,500	0.06	$ 149,670.84
2033	$5,500	0.06	$ 164,481.09
2034	$5,500	0.06	$ 180,179.95
2035	$5,500	0.06	$ 196,820.75
2036	$5,500	0.06	$ 214,460.00
2037	$5,500	0.06	$ 233,157.60
2038	$6,500	0.06	$ 254,037.05
2039	$6,500	0.06	$ 276,169.28
2040	$6,500	0.06	$ 299,629.43
2041	$6,500	0.06	$ 324,497.20
2042	$6,500	0.06	$ 350,857.03
2043	$6,500	0.06	$ 378,798.45
2044	$6,500	0.06	$ 408,416.36
2045	$6,500	0.06	$ 439,811.34
2046	$6,500	0.06	$ 473,090.02
2047	$6,500	0.06	$ 508,365.42
2048	$6,500	0.06	$ 545,757.35
2049	$6,500	0.06	$ 585,392.79
2050	$6,500	0.06	$ 627,406.36
2051	$6,500	0.06	$ 671,940.74
2052	$6,500	0.06	$ 719,147.18

With 6 percent annual compounding, maxing contributions to a Roth IRA over 35 years gets you almost $720,000 at age 65. Best of all that money can now be taken out *tax free*. In addition, there are no RMDs for you. You don't have to take the money out at 70½, or ever for that matter. And while it would still count towards any estate taxes, when someone inherits your Roth IRA, they could take out the whole amount without any income taxes.

There is also an option to convert some or all of a traditional IRA into a Roth IRA. Because of the tax free growth, our clients occasionally look at converting some traditional IRA funds into a Roth IRA and just pay the taxes. This becomes a particularly valuable proposition if the non-tax-deferred money they had in the stock market crashed in a particular year and they have some losses they can write off. In those years, why not add some to your taxable income if it is going to be offset, and the end result is you get a whole bunch of money now growing tax free?

There is quite a bit more we can discuss regarding tax-deferred accounts in the financial planning context, let alone in the estate planning context. For more information on the estate planning aspects of inheriting retirement accounts, please see my book *The IRA Trust*, available at www.PlainEnglishAttorney.com.

Chapter Five:
Banking and Government-Backed Investments

Ross and Jennifer were as conservative in their investing as they could be. They were a huge fan of banks, and hated to have anything at risk in the stock market. While they were in their early 50s, they grew up with big hardship stories from their grandparents and great grandparents who scraped along to get by after the stock market crash and the Great Depression. With a lot of thanks to President Roosevelt and banking protections, the next four generations stayed far away from any risk and only trusted banks.

But now they were starting to look at huge periods of very little interest, to the point that they felt they were actually losing ground while their peers were getting ahead.

"I just don't trust the market," Jennifer said emphatically. "I can't afford to lose what we've worked so hard to build. But I'm starting to feel like I'm paying the bank to keep my money rather than my bank paying me interest."

"Unfortunately, that feeling is something I'm hearing a lot of from my clients," I told them. "Bank accounts and bank investments have a place in a solid financial plan, but for most people, it shouldn't be the entire financial plan."

"But it needs to be safe," Ross said. "Having our money in banks that are FDIC insured means we can't lose our money. And with the limit raised to $250,000, we can keep our life savings comfortably spread out over 7 banks with some room to spare."

I heard about FDIC insurance a lot when talking to clients. Unfortunately, it isn't all it's cracked up to be, and I started explaining this to Ross and Jennifer. "Let's be clear about what FDIC insurance covers and how it works," I said. "Banks that are FDIC insured doesn't mean that the bank won't fail or go under. It does means that if the bank does go under that the federal government will get you your money back. But it may take a few days. However, when we look at how little interest is being paid on your money compared to some other safe investments, you are actually giving up quite a bit to make sure that the federal government is insuring your deposit."

"But where else are you going to get your money insured like a bank?" Jennifer asked.

"Actually, life insurance and some annuities are often guaranteed by state governments," I said. "And you don't have to give up nearly as much just to make sure your money is government-insured. North Carolina currently protects up to $300,000."

That seemed to take them aback. "Now, I'm not advocating getting rid of all of your bank accounts, or even getting rid of your CDs if you are hanging on to some older ones with great interest," I said. "But usually my clients keep a certain amount liquid in checking and money market accounts, but then put the money they consider 'investment money' into annuities to get better, but still guaranteed safe, growth. Here are some things we can look at to make your financial plan a little more well-rounded..."

Most of my clients want the security of an FDIC insured bank, but at the same time they want to earn a lot more than banks are typically paying. But that doesn't mean that banking accounts and instruments don't have a place in a financial plan, and it is important to make sure that you understand at least the basics of what banks offer.

For many of my clients, it makes sense to have some money that is 100% liquid and accessible, and this usually happens through the "main three" accounts with banks: checking, savings, and money market accounts. This may even just be true for holding enough money to pay the monthly bills plus maybe a month or two of cushion, and that's it.

Checking Accounts

Ever since I was 14, I had a checking account to put away the money I earned in my summer job. Of course, at that age a parent had to sign and be responsible for the account until I turned eighteen. And this is often how many Americans are first involved in banking. The vast majority of people maintain some kind of checking account, mainly for deposits coming in and bills being paid going out.

Because of this functionality and numerous transactions, there is often very little interest, if any, paid on money in checking accounts. In fact, some accounts, depending on the balance you keep, have fees that will actually decrease your balance each month so you have the privilege of being able to pay your bills. Because of this, checking accounts are not often seen as "investment" bank accounts.

Savings Accounts

As the name implies, savings accounts are where people accumulate their savings, and there may not necessarily be a lot of transactions with savings accounts each month. Many people use savings accounts as a place to store their "extra" money left over when their paycheck exceeds the amount of their bills each month. The excess money is then transferred from the checking account to the savings account.

Now that there is sometimes money accumulating in the savings account but not a lot of transactions, banks are often providing a greater rate of interest compared to checking accounts. However, the amount of interest is still considered miniscule compared to other investments out there. What people like about savings accounts is not that it has some kind of fantastic interest rate; it's that their money is liquid, FDIC insured (to a limit), and making just a bit more interest than zero.

Just as a point of interest, credit unions typically do not have "savings accounts" but rather the exact same type of account is called a "share" account, and it is this deposit that represents a person's "membership" interest in the credit union. Essentially for investment purposes they are the same thing, with the one exception that credit unions require you to have a small balance in a share account (sometimes only $25) in order to conduct any other business with them, but banks do not require a savings account in order to have checking accounts or CDs with them.

Money Market Accounts

While many people look at money market deposit accounts like checking accounts with greater interest, it is technically classified as a savings account with variable interest rates. As interest rates for borrowing and lending fluctuate, so does the interest on money market accounts. In general, this usually results in higher gains than savings accounts, but there are also typically some restrictions:

- Higher minimum balances are needed to avoid fees and to get the better interest rates.
- There are often limits on the number of withdrawals each month without incurring service charges of about $10 per transaction.
- Excessive transactions may also result in the account being closed.

The still small but better interest rates for money market accounts often means that people who have enough to meet the minimum balance requirements will put their "FDIC-insured safe money" in a money market account over a savings account. And rates for money market accounts can vary greatly between banks, to the point that some banks may be offering money market rates that are much better than certificates of deposit (CDs) that have severe restrictions on accessing the money.

Certificates of Deposit

Long considered the best "guaranteed safe" investment, certificates of deposit, or CDs, pay a guaranteed interest rate provided you lock in your deposit for a set period of time. And usually, the longer the time period the money is locked in, the better the interest rate. But even so, CD rates have become so low that people are generally avoiding them as investments because the interest rates are not even keeping up with inflation, even with historically low inflation.

"With interest rates like that, I might as well deposit my cash into my sock drawer," I'll hear clients tell me. And they are not wrong. As you'll see in later chapters, there are some better, guaranteed safe investments that people are taking advantage of.

One exception to the usually parsimonious interest rates are much older certificates of deposit that banks issued long ago but have guaranteed renewal clauses that allow you to keep renewing the same CD with the good interest rate. I have seen some clients with CDs with 4% or even 5% interest that they have just kept renewing for every six months for more than 20 years. But these are definitely the exception rather than the rule.

For all four of these general types of bank products, the one thing that we often hear when people keep large sums of money in them is they feel comfortable because the bank is FDIC insured. But what, exactly, does that mean?

Federal Deposit Insurance Corporation (FDIC)

The Federal Deposit Insurance Corporation, or commonly just referred to as FDIC, is a federally chartered business that insures deposits that people make in member banks. There is actually no taxpayer money funding it, but banks pay their insurance "premiums" to support FDIC and its insuring functions, but the FDIC also has a line of credit available with the U.S. Treasury Department for up to $100 billion. If a bank goes under, then all of the depositors are insured up to $250,000. (In fact, there are several different account categories that depositors can have their money in and be insured, and it is actually $250,000 *per depositor per category*.) In addition, while banks and credit unions are often thought of as being the same thing, credit unions are not part of the FDIC system but instead have the same types of rules and limits but under the National Credit Union Administration.

It is this insurance protection that many people desire to keep their money guaranteed safe, and many people keep the bulk of their money in banks because of these guarantees. And when people have more money than the $250,000 in their preferred type of account, they will simply start a new bank account at another institution in order to stay under the FDIC insurance limits.

Many years ago, when the limit was at $100,000 rather than $250,000, my law firm assisted with the probate estate of a couple who had about $1.6 million each spread out over multiple banks so no one account went over the $100,000 limit. In all, there were about 35 or so bank accounts at 19 different banks, all in savings accounts. Yes, it was all guaranteed safe and liquid, but over the years they missed out on quite a bit of growth and interest that still could have been guaranteed safe through life insurance and annuity options. As you already read, state governments will often insure annuities and life insurance up to certain amounts just like FDIC but can pay out significantly more over the long run.

Chapter Six: Real Estate

Todd and Vickie has the cutest grandson, and they brought him to their appointment. After all, he was one of the reasons they had to update their estate and financial plans. Their daughter Carol went through some terrible ordeals, and she just couldn't keep her son anymore and get her life together at the same time. So guardianship had passed to the two people in the world she could depend on to raise her son the way she wanted, and that was her parents.

"We never thought we'd be raising a child at our age," Todd said. "We figured that was over almost a decade ago. But family does what it has to."

It was clear that they were enjoying time with their grandson, but this meant there was a lot more they had to consider. Of course, Todd and Vickie had to think about guardianship for their grandson, and we discussed several nieces and nephews who would be up to the task should anything happen to both of them. But then we did have to get into the financial commitment they were taking on. At the moment, they had more than enough income to cover their own retirement costs and that of raising their grandson, but the "big ticket" items were not here yet. College is very expensive, and it doesn't seem to be getting any better. So where was the income coming from?

Real estate.

Todd was doing very well holding almost a dozen rental properties, some with mortgages and others without, and they were all rented at the moment. But Vickie was not nearly as involved as Todd was in the real estate business, although her background in accounting would probably serve her well. Todd was starting to show her more and more of his real estate business, just in case anything happened to him. They were both a little surprised when I asked a simple question.

"Vickie, do you <u>want</u> to handle the real estate if anything happens to Todd?" I asked. "We might be able to do the same or even better for income if we sell off and reinvest the proceeds. Plus if anything happens to both of you, there would be more than enough liquid assets for your grandson to go to college without having to manage your real estate holdings at the same time."

"Oh," Todd said. "He'd never have the time to be a full time college student if he had to do what I do to keep the rent coming in on time."

"Exactly," I said. "Let's take a look at some other options."

Real estate is often a sound investment, depending on how much you want to leverage your real estate holdings with mortgages. And if your intent is to rent out property and be a landlord, it could take a substantial amount of time. It's nice when the rent checks come in, and some of our clients enjoy being property holders, but others became landlords by default because they couldn't sell a second home when they wanted to because of bad market conditions. Real estate on its own is very illiquid, and you may be stuck holding unrented real estate with a mortgage payment you can't afford.

This chapter will review the basics of some of the real estate options out there. But first, I often have discussions with clients who end up complaining that the value of their home or vacation property has gone down. "I checked around, and my house lost about 30% of its value in the last crash nine years ago and it hasn't even gotten back to its pre-crash value yet," I hear. "That's terrible!"

"So what?" I never actually ask, but it really does get to the heart of my next point. If you aren't selling the real estate in the near future, why do you care?

Real estate values only matter if you are looking to sell or if you are using the property as collateral for a loan. Unless you are in one of these two situations, you are simply using the property to live your life. The purpose of the property is *habitation*, not investing. In fact, lower property values can often be transformed into lower property taxes. Some of my clients have successfully challenged their real estate property tax bills based on a real estate crash (or one that has not fully recovered) in order to get a lower tax bill. In North Carolina, property valuations are made by the county at least every ten years, but in any given year there are procedures for appealing your tax bill based on the real value of the property. It can be argued that you actually *want* your property values to be lower if you don't intend to sell or borrow.

Provided you are looking to buy and sell real estate, or borrow against real estate for other investments, what kind of general real estate it out there?

Residential Real Estate

The most common form of real estate investments my clients have is residential real estate, either to rent out for income purposes or to buy and sell. In both cases, these are home for people to live in rather than office workplaces, manufacturing or retail/wholesale stores. Because these are places for people to live, there are often state, county, and possibly municipal laws and regulations you have to obey. Property conditions often have to legally meet certain minimum standards that are much higher than commercial property, at least for the investor.

Some of our clients who hold and rent residential real estate find it much easier to simply hire a property manager or company that will collect the rent, manage and then deduct any repair expenses, and essentially handle the entire leasing process with the exception of getting approval for large expenses, such as a new central air conditioning system. While this makes life much more convenient for the property owners, the companies do get paid for what they do, and those costs need to be incorporated into the investment.

When it comes to buying and selling real estate, there are often far more costs than people initially assume. Good money can be made from buying houses at a lower cost and then selling them for a much higher cost, but there is often a lot of renovations involved. The typical process is to 1) buy the property, often with a mortgage, 2) use money to renovate and overhaul the property to make it much more attractive, and then 3) sell the property at a significant profit even after you pay back the mortgage. Sometimes, investors also borrow the money to make the upgrades before selling.

Sounds great! But there are some potential downsides. If you underestimate the cost of the repairs and renovations, you may inadvertently end up wiping out your profit margin and lose money on the deal. There may also be severe delays in the renovations and repairs if the contractor is backed up, and in the meantime you are paying a mortgage that is almost all interest, again reducing or wiping out your profit margin. And finally, if there is a severe downturn in the market, or you just are not able to sell quickly, then you can also wipe out your profit margin or lose money.

Playing the residential real estate game can yield big profits, but it can also take up a lot of time, effort, and worry only to lose money in the end. For most of my clients at or near retirement, these are risks they just don't want to deal with.

Commercial Real Estate

In general, commercial real estate is a lot easier to deal with than residential real estate, but it is also much more susceptible to economic downturns than residential real estate. After all, no matter how bad the economy gets people will still need a place to live, whether it is owning or renting. But if the demand for the products and services businesses provide are down, then the businesses are not going to rent or buy the commercial property.

So what makes commercial real estate easier to "deal with" compared to residential? In my more than 20 years of practicing law, I have found a huge difference between residential leasing and commercial leasing. For residential leasing, there are any number of responsibilities on the landlord that are mandatory under state and federal law. While there are many laws and regulations related to business workplaces and stores, arguably even more than residential real estate, the burden of complying with those regulations is on the *business*, not *the landlord.*

For example, commercial leases often have clauses shifting the responsibility for plumbing fixtures and water damage to the business leasing the property, and the responsibility for things like water mains and sewage pipes at the point of leaving the building are on the landlord to fix. In a residential rental, the toilets, sinks, and other plumbing is solely on the landlord to keep in good working order.

What I have found for most of my clients, though, is that they only really want to deal with the headaches and financial risks of leasing commercial property, or buying and selling it, is if they are in the full-time business of commercial real estate. If they are only looking for investments, commercial real estate tends to not be one of the things they want to "dabble" in.

Real Estate Investment Trusts (REITs)

There is an investment designed to take advantage of the potential upsides of the real estate market while spreading the risk out among different properties and pooling investors called a Real Estate Investment Trust, often called a REIT.

The concept is pretty simple. The REIT pulls together a group of investors and their money so they can buy more real estate than any one person alone could. By purchasing multiple properties, the REIT also reduces the impact of any one or two properties not being rented or being on the market and not sold for a significant amount of time. And now the law of averages makes it more cost effective to own multiple properties, and, on average, you'll earn a more steady return on your money without the huge risk of owning a property that won't sell or won't lease.

Of course, there are some downsides. Just because you are lumped in with a large group of investors doesn't mean there is a guarantee you won't lose money. A huge hit to the real estate market means that the REIT may also lose money you have invested, and it may take years for it to come back. And a big sale of major assets is great for the REIT, but your profit is only the proportion the REIT pays out, and if the managers of the REIT decide to reinvest the money into another property, you only typically have a say in proportion to your ownership percentage (if then).

Yes, REITs do have their downsides, but for many of my clients it's a better way to invest in real estate if you don't want to be a full time landlord, or invest in residential or commercial properties all on your own.

Annuity-Based Real Estate Index Investing

One type of real estate investing that is quickly growing popular is investing in a real estate index as part of an indexed annuity. These annuities allow you to share in the upsides of the real estate market during a certain period, but at the same time you are not subject to losses during that period. In other words, the worst that happens is your investment stays the same even if the real estate market tanks.

We'll go into more detail on this option later when we discuss fixed and indexed annuities, but for now the general concept is that your investment is actually part of an insurance contract where the insurance company agrees to increase your money based on the real estate market index over a set period of time and according to specific parameters. Some of those parameters may be that your gains are capped at a certain level, or that you only get a certain percentage of the upside, or even that you pay a certain percentage of the gain to the company first and then all of the rest of the gains are yours. The big factors in all of this for many of my senior clients are:

- They don't have to be landlords to make money on real estate rentals.
- They don't have to worry about losing money on a real estate sale or pay money on a mortgage for a property that doesn't sell.
- And unlike a REIT, they are guaranteed not to lose money.

With all of these factors, quite a few people are looking at these indexed annuities as a way to take advantage of the real estate market without the risk of losing their shirt.

The real estate market has many pros and cons for investors, with some big potential paydays. But how you invest in real estate depends a lot on how much time you want to invest as well as how much risk you want to take on. And those factors are more often than not directly related to your particular stage of life and how much time you have before you need your investment proceeds to live. However, there are ways of investing in real estate that may be appropriate for your situation, and real estate investing in general shouldn't be dismissed out of hand.

Chapter Seven: Stocks, Bonds, and Mutual Funds

The death of a long-time estate planning client is never easy, and George was no different. He was one of the smartest, well-researched clients we had, and he always looked into things to understand all of his different options, but then moved quickly once he made up his mind. When we made the last adjustments to his and his wife's estate plan, George made it plain to me that his wife Janice and his son Kelly were going to need a lot of help on the financial end of things. "They just don't understand the stock market the way I do," he confided in me. "I don't think they can keep things going the way I do. Please tell me you'll help them even if it means staying out of the market. I just want to make sure that Janice is taken care of after I'm gone."

And George was right. There were many financial advisors and stock brokers who relied on their main offices, mutual fund managers, and other sources to come up with diversified portfolios to lessen risk but still have bigger potentials for gains. But George spent about 25 hours a week doing his own research on companies, and he frequently instructed his broker to sell certain stocks when he saw the company tanking in the near future, or to buy stocks for a company that he felt was undervalued in the market. To George's credit, he was able to outperform most brokers and financial advisors because he put in an extensive amount of time and thought.

This is what made things so difficult when I had a meeting with Janice and Kelly after George passed on. It was time to retool the way their investments were held, but they didn't see why it was necessary.

"But dad always did well in the stock market," Kelly said. "He understood the market and always made a lot of money. Why would we change things? It doesn't make sense."

"Your dad understood the market, and he put in a lot of time doing the research necessary to get those gains," I told Kelly and Janice. "He was very knowledgeable, did his homework, and stayed on top of things every day. Do you understand the market the way he does? Are you willing to devote about 25 hours a week to making sure you aren't making any mistakes?"

"I don't have an extra 25 hours a week," Kelly said.

"Exactly," I said. "Janice, isn't that about how much time George spent every week?"

"At least," Janice said. "I'd sit and do my knitting and watch my shows, or just read, and George would be right there with me in the family room on the computer looking over annual reports and other stuff. It was what he liked to do since he retired, but I could never get into it that much."

"But I've always been told that stocks are always the best way to grow money," Kelly said. "I have my money in stocks with my broker."

"Yes, over the long term, stocks can make you more money," I replied. "But your mom is 73. She can't afford to lose a bunch of money in the stock market without jeopardizing her lifestyle. Plus she's told me she wants to travel more and spend time with the grandchildren, and that will actually cost money. She can't do that if the market crashes, but she can if her money is guaranteed safe but still making more than bank CD rates."

"That sounds good to me," Janice said. "George did want me to make sure you were helping us after he was gone, and I can see why."

"Does this mean I should be talking to my broker about taking my money out of the stock market?" Kelly asked.

"You should always talk to your broker," I told Kelly. "But you're in your mid-forties, and you have twenty years until retirement. It might be time to start moving some of your investments out of the market, but not necessarily all of it. You don't need to have your investments handled like your mom's because you have different goals and circumstances right now. Janice can't afford to invest like she could in her forties, but you might be losing out if you invest like you are in your seventies. Let's see if we can figure out what is best for your mom separate from what might be best for you."

The stock market has some big potential for gains, but it also has a huge potential for losses. And there are different ways to be invested in stocks, with some ways being far more risky (and potentially rewarding) than others. There are lots of facts and figures showing that the market "always comes back" and provide gains, but timing is everything. And I'm not talking about timing the market, but how much time you have before you need your money.

This is why many of my clients look to decrease the percentage of their portfolio invested in stocks as they grow older, and they often decease the level of risk in the types of stocks chosen. They then shift the investments into less risky or even guaranteed safe investments so their money will be there when they need it. So what are the main types of stock investing out there?

Brokerage Accounts

By far the most risky type of stock investing, this is an account where you can pick and choose stocks, and the value of the brokerage account rises and falls with the value of those stocks. I've seen many brokerage accounts in my years as an estate planning, and most have about 20-30 different company stocks. The types of stocks can range from safer, "blue chip" stocks to risky stocks on emerging companies that might or might not make it big. In general, if any three stocks tank, so will your brokerage account. If two or three stocks take off and none of the others lose, or at least not lose too badly, then your account may have a good year. But in a bad year, if 17 of your 20 evenly distributed stocks don't go anywhere and three companies completely go under, that's a 15% loss in your portfolio. Many of my clients don't want that level of risk, even seeing that if the opposite *might* come true and they get a 15% gain in any one year.

Mutual Funds

While less risky, mutual funds are still at risk in the market, but much less so. At least in theory. Mutual funds aren't the same as brokerage accounts where you directly own stocks. Instead, a company will create a fund that invests in hundreds (or possibly thousands) of different corporations, and you buy shares of that fund.

This lessens the potential risk of a few, or even a dozen, companies faltering and having your investments go into a tailspin. Mutual funds are designed to try to gain more than the overall stock market, but at the same time eliminate companies that the fund managers believe are more risky. However, doing this does make the mutual fund more vulnerable when the overall economy goes down, or it can increase as the overall economy grows.

Just as there are more and less aggressive stocks to invest in, there are also more and less aggressive mutual funds comprising different weighted balances of stocks. Some mutual funds are more vested in international stocks than domestic. Some stocks are more invested in technology fields, and others are more weighted towards real estate and other "hard" assets. But the common factors they all have is they are not guaranteed safe, and they can gain or lose your money.

Bonds

By far the safest of investments that are still "in the market," bonds are promises by companies and municipalities to pay back loans with interest. So people are not actually investing in a company and getting a portion of ownership (or owning a piece of a town or city). But they are buying into the company's promise to repay the loan.

The reason bonds tend to be safer are by holding a bond, you are actually an unsecured creditor of the company or municipality and therefore have a legal right to be repaid before stockholders should the company declare bankruptcy. However, your right as a bondholder to get paid comes after any *secured* loan holders, such as the company getting a mortgage on a building or a company pledging assets as collateral for the loan. The company can *still* go under, and can *still* lose some or all of your investment in that bond.

When it comes to municipalities, the risk tends to be a little less, but the payout also tends to be a little less. Basically, you are lending a city, town, or county money for certain operating expenses, and the municipality agrees to pay you back. One of the more attractive aspects of municipal bonds is even though they do tend to pay out less, there are many municipal bonds where the interest paid is tax free, potentially off-setting the lower rate of return for investors.

In general, far more companies declare bankruptcy and default on their bonds than government entities do, but it is not unheard of. There were several municipalities that declared bankruptcy during the Great Recession of 2008-2009, and investors did lose their money.

Indexed Annuities

One of more popular ways of "riding the coattails" of the stock market for seniors is to have their money in indexed annuities rather than directly in stocks. The concept is similar to the section on real estate indexes. Basically, you don't own any stocks, but an insurance company contracts with you to have your money grow while "tied" to specific market indexes while guaranteeing against losses in the market. And more and more each year, the choices seem to be expanding. We'll discuss this in more detail in the specific chapter on annuities, but here are some of the basic items to look for:

- The Computation Period. There are set dates to look at when computing the value of your indexed annuity. For many, it is a specific start and end date during a calendar year, but the date can be one year apart, two years apart, or even three years apart. (I'm sure there are some that might be more.) There are also some that are computed monthly, but for these be sure to look at the fine print and the "caps" on the gains and losses each month.

- Number of years of the annuity. In most cases, there is a set amount of time in which access to your money without some kind of penalty or charge is limited. Just like with bank CDs, the longer your money is "tied up," the more favorable the interest and growth typically is. For example, ten year annuities (a fairly standard term) will provide better terms than a three or five year annuity. While that sounds like a long time to be unable to access your money, most, if not all, of these annuities allow you to take out up to ten percent of your investment each year without any penalties or surrender charges. This becomes particularly important when building in liquidity for potential long term care expenses or Medicaid nursing home cases inside irrevocable trusts; we always want to make sure that there is more than enough money liquid to handle medical costs, so we factor in the possible withdrawal of ten percent per year for five years in a way that can cover costs before Medicaid would kick in if health conditions take a turn for the worse.

- Caps and Participation Rates. The amount of growth for an indexed annuity varies from company to company, and often has what are known as "caps" and "participation rates. A cap simply means that there is a maximum limit to the amount of growth the annuity company will provide during the specific time period. For example, if the annuity is tied to the S&P 500 but is "capped" at 11%, that means that if the S&P 500 grows 14% that your account will only be credited for 11%.

Participation rates are also common, meaning there is a set percentage of the increases that your annuity account will credit to you. For example, in the same S&P 500 growth of 15%, if you have a "90% participation rate," then that means that your account will get 90% of the 15% growth, or 12.6% growth (.15 x .9=.126). It is also possible that there might be a combination of the two, so that the same 15% growth may be capped at 11% and have a 90% participation rate, so when faced with the 12.6% growth, you investment would actually be capped at the 11% figure so you would just get the 11%.

- The Index. There are also many different indexes that the annuity can be tied to, with the most popular being the S&P 500. However, it can also be tied to the Dow or the Nasdaq, to name a few more. It is important to understand each one of these indexes and how the index itself might be weighted when choosing an indexed annuity. For example, the Nasdaq may be much more heavily weighted to technology stocks, so if there is a boom or bust in the technology industry, it will impact your indexed annuity much more than an S&P 500 Indexed annuity.

While there are many different ways of investing in stocks that impact the degree of risk you are taking, the one consistent factor is that when you invest directly in stocks you run the risk of losing your money. Investing in brokerage accounts may be a little more risky than investing in bonds, but there is still the possibility of losing your investment. The one exception is technically not investing IN stocks, but being tied to the performance of a stock-based index with a guarantee not to lose money through indexed annuities.

Chapter Eight:
Fixed Assets

Back in 2009, I sat down with Patty, a 67 year old widow who had been on her own since her husband died ten years ago. We had just finished up signing her estate planning documents when she started to ask me about investing in gold.

"I just got this in the mail yesterday," she said, handing over a three page, front-and-back report on the benefits of investing in gold. "I'm really thinking I should put my money in gold since the stock market has been so bad lately."

I understood completely. Unfortunately, Patty had ignored the advice from a year and a half ago to move about 75% of her money from stocks to something guaranteed safe and to move her remaining 25% in stocks from moderate to conservative. Now, with a significantly lessened portfolio, Patty was looking for a silver bullet.

"Patty, that's really not a good idea right now," I told her.

"But just take a look at how well gold has performed!" she said, practically shoving the report into my hands. "Gold has skyrocketed in the last six months!"

"That's because the economy has tanked," I told her. "In general, gold goes up when the economy is weak because people fear an economic collapse. The reason gold is so valuable right now is because everything crashed in the last six months. If you get into the gold market now, you're just buying at a high rate. The value of gold tends to go down when the economy improves, so you're just likely to see the money you invest now go down as the economy improves."

"So you mean there's no hope for me to make my money back?" Patty said.

"It would take quite a while to come back," I said. "And it's even more difficult now because you don't have as much money to invest. Gold is a great hedge against an economy falling, but you have to have it before the economy falls apart. Let's see what other options are out there…"

No review of investing basics would be complete without looking at gold and other fixed assets. A few people do invest heavily in antiques, artwork, precious metals, and other "hard" assets. Depending on what is considered valuable at the time, different kinds of hard assets can grow considerably in value. For example, a painter who has died may have the value of their work skyrocket because their life story was just featured in a major motion picture. Or in the case of a down economy, gold tends to make people feel more secure than cash or stocks, so people buy up gold making it more scarce and valuable.

But in the end, there are several things to keep in mind when deciding whether or not to invest in these different kinds of hard assets:

- Unless it is something sold on an open market, hard assets tend to be fairly illiquid and may take months or years to sell at its true value. A rare, antique writing desk belonging to one of the Founding Fathers may be worth hundreds of thousands of dollars to the right collector. But the right collector might not be able or willing to pay full price at that particular time. However, they may be willing a year or two later. An exception to this is that there are some "accounts" that hold precious metals that are regularly bought and sold. In most of these cases, you don't actually have the physical gold on hand.

- Trends may impact your particular hard investments more than anything else, and therefore your investment may be subject to whim. In the late 90s, Beanie Babies were all the rage, and serious collectors would buy and sell these stuffed animals for outrageous sums for the rarest of them. In some cases, there was even fraud around "fake" Beanie Babies being sold to unsuspecting buyers. But given a few years and trends changing, the market for Beanie Babies went away, along with all of the money collectors invested. There are still some collectors out there, but because trends changed, the value of the investment changed dramatically.

- Hard assets may also be extremely hard to value. Anyone who has seen the television program Antique Roadshow can tell you that one person's junk may turn into something extremely rare and valuable. But even some items may have varied values associated with it depending on the person doing the appraising. And even more unfortunately, the person doing the appraising may turn out to be a potential buyer who now has an incentive to lowball the value, prompting another appraisal. And independent appraisals cost money.

- Finally, geography may limit the pool of prospective buyers. At least for the bigger stuff. When it comes to things like coin collections, comic books, or baseball cards, photos can be fairly easily used to communicate with prospective buyers around the world. But when it comes to antique furniture, many buyers want to inspect the item in person, particularly if it will cost tens or hundreds of thousands of dollars. And there may not be a lot of people willing to make the trip to visually inspect an item with an eye towards buying it.

In general, most of my clients shy away from investing in hard assets with the notable exception of precious metals like gold and silver. This is mainly because they don't suffer from the four downsides listed that many other hard assets do. Gold and silver are openly traded, and you can look up the value online on a daily basis. Trends don't really impact the value of gold and silver (although the economy does). There's no real need for appraisals since precious metals are sold by weight and purity; there is very little subjectivity there. And finally, geography is not really a concern because there is 1) almost always someone willing to buy precious metals nearby, or 2) it can simply be sold on the open market.

However, the value still fluctuates with the economy and the market for precious metals. It is still possible to lose money by investing directly in precious metals. But there is a way to invest in gold without actually purchasing it, much in the same way people can put their money into an indexed annuity that is "tied" to the market without suffering the potential losses.

Although we'll discuss it in more detail later, there are some indexed annuities that offer an option of tying your investment to the gold market. As with the other indexed annuity provisions, it is guaranteed not to lose money in the gold market, but at the same time there may be participation percentages and caps. When my clients understand that gold and other precious metals grow in the face of a falling economy, they look at the gold option in an indexed annuity as a "hedge against the market." In other words, they may only have a portion of their investment in gold so that if the economy goes down, that gold investment may tend to go up. At the same time, they also have some (or even most) of the investment in the indexed annuity tied to stocks and/or real estate, so if the economy goes up the gold portion would probably stay even and not grow while the other investments probably grow.

While having investments in fixed assets, and particularly precious metals, can be lucrative if you *really* know what you are doing, there are ways to use these kinds of assets to your advantage without actually directly owning them.

Chapter Nine:
Annuities

"I've read more about annuities, and I understand that not all annuities are the same," Carl said. "I think at my age some kind of annuity is probably a good fit for the money I want to keep safe. But I'm really not sure what I should be looking for. All I know is that I don't want to lose money in the market, but at the same time bank CD rates are horrible."

Carl was like a lot of my senior clients, either in retirement or close to it. At 63, he wanted to make sure that his investments were appropriately safe for his retirement, but having an interest rate that didn't even keep up with inflation was not acceptable. I know we can do a little better.

"I know we can find something, or a few somethings, that are right for your situation," I told Carl. "The thing is that there are many, many different types of annuities with numerous combinations of terms and features. But let's first try to narrow down the main types of annuities out there, check out some of the different features of the different types, and then decide what gets you where you want to go. The very general types are fixed, indexed, variable, and then there are different markets and indexes to look at."

"So there aren't just one or two annuities out there," Carl joked. "It sounds complicated, but that's why I'm talking to you."

"That's the problem when there are a ton of choices," I joked back. "With so many different options to choose from, making a decision is not always easy. But what we try to do is figure out what you like and don't like, and then find what fits best with your goals. In other words, tell us what you like and we'll put together a few options."

"Now that sounds a lot easier!" Carl said.

"Great," I said. "Here are the main types and what they do…"

Carl's situation is not unique. Many of our clients have been diligently putting money away in their 401ks, investing in whatever their broker advised, and now that they are getting closer to retirement, they are really starting to pay more attention. Before, they were OK with the "just let it ride in the market" mentality because they were earning enough income through their jobs. But now that retirement is looming, they need to make sure that their assets will be enough that they don't run out of money. Often annuities are an option our clients turn to because they like that they are guaranteed safe, but they also want to understand the basics of what they are and how they work.

The main types out there fixed annuities, indexed annuities, and variable annuities, or some combination of those. There are also single premium immediate annuities, and there is also an explanation needed for a big feature called the "income accumulation" account in the variable annuity section.

Fixed Annuities

By far, the easiest annuities to understand are fixed annuities because they often work a lot like bank CDs. You make a deposit of your money, and it is guaranteed to make a fixed amount of interest over a specific period of time. And, usually, the longer the time period, the greater the interest rate. As with just about all annuities, there are penalties and fees if you take the money out early, but even fixed annuities will allow you to take out up to ten percent (10%) each year without them. Of course, this does mean that the money you took out is no longer making interest, so it is usually best to make sure what you are putting into a fixed annuity is very likely to just stay there for the whole time period, barring any unforeseen financial needs.

There are also some fixed annuities that are not necessarily totally "fixed." In other words, there is a minimum fixed interest rate, but depending on the insurance company's performance, it may actually issue a higher interest rate for a particular year. In these cases, it is always important to see the company's track record of interest. Our office also tends to be very conservative when it comes to these matters, and we often stress that, at the very least, you should be happy if the company only paid the guaranteed fixed interest rate before getting such an annuity.

Indexed Annuities

As I mentioned earlier in the book, indexed annuities are *tied* to market performance without having to actually *own* stocks in the stock market. Basically, you don't own any stocks, but an insurance company contracts with you to have your money grow while "tied" to specific market indexes while guaranteeing against losses in the market. And more and more each year, the choices seem to be expanding. For many of my clients, indexed annuities are the perfect investing intersection of their money being guaranteed safe but with a large potential to grow.

While there are any number of indexes to look at, the main one is usually the Standard and Poor's 500 (S&P 500) because it has been the most consistently performing index over long periods of time. Unless there is some specific reason or desire on the part of our clients for something different, such as wanting a smaller or greater percentage in international investments, the usual market index the annuity is tied to is the S&P 500. This is regardless of the particular annuity company or annuity terms. Because there are so many choices and differing parameters when it comes to finding out what type of indexed annuity is right for a particular client (and because things can change pretty quickly in the annuity market), I don't want to list them here. We can always look at your particular situation a lot more closely if you wish and then find some very specific recommendations for your very specific needs and goals. However, as promised, we will go into more detail later in this chapter in the "One Popular Solution" section.

Variable Annuities

While covered in more detail earlier, we want to make sure the option of variable annuities is at least mentioned in this section. A variable annuity actually *does* have your money invested *in* the stock market directly, and your investment is not just tied to the market. To make sure we are covering it again, in our opinion variable annuities have the following characteristics as they relate to our clients:

- There is a risk of loss, so variable annuities are usually more appropriate for the money you are OK risking in the stock market.

- Most of our clients would rather simply invest in the stock market rather than in a variable annuity if their goal is to grow their money.

- The big exception to this rule is that variable annuities can be tremendously advantageous if the ultimate goal is to "turn on" the annuity so it becomes a stream of income since most of the guarantees associated with variable annuities relate to what is known as the "income accumulation" section of the annuity contract. When an annuity has two tracked "values," it is usually that one method of tracking is how the investment is actually doing in the market if you decided to cash it out, but the other method is a different amount, and this is the value of the annuity should you decide to turn it into the income stream, otherwise known as "annuitizing" it. Because the income accumulation portion usually has guarantees and the regular investment portion often has fees deducted, it is common for variable annuities to have the income accumulation portion grow much larger than the actual investment account portion's value.

When we have clients who are at or near retirement, they are not usually interested in starting a variable annuity, but if they already have one the usual discussion is not around *whether* to turn it into an income stream but *when*. Either that, or we end up discussing how and when to get out of the variable annuity because the risk factor is becoming more than our clients want as they grow older.

Single Premium Immediate Annuities (SPIAs)

Sometimes, part of proper financial planning is more about making sure that there is a guaranteed stream of income coming in rather than growing the nest egg. And in other cases, there may be a specific need to reduce assets but increase income for one member of a married couple for Medicaid or other benefits planning. These situations can involve what is called a single premium immediate annuity, or a "SPIA" for short.

The concept is simple but with a lot of choices. Basically, you can take a lump sum of money to an annuity company, and they can then turn around and provide you an agreed upon stream of income. The income can last for the rest of your life (however long that is), for a specific period of time, or even for the remainder of your life with a guaranteed minimum number of years.

Most of our clients who express interest in SPIAs usually have longevity in their family, they have accumulated a lot in assets, but they don't have enough income to suit their desired standard of living. So they often want to look at options about having income for life rather than a finite amount of assets that could dwindle and become depleted during their life. Depending on the situation, this may be a safer and more worry-free route for our clients than trying to keep growing assets hoping they won't run out before they pass on.

One Popular Solution

More and more, our clients who want their money to be guaranteed safe but also want to earn money really like the various, multiple annuity options. They like the fixed portion because there is a predictable interest rate (or at least a predictable minimum interest rate). They also like the real estate investment option without having to actually own the real estate. They like the potential returns of an indexed annuity without the risk of actually having their money in the market. And they like the security of hedging against a potential downturn in the market by having some of their money invested in gold. So what do we do with all of these competing desires?

In the past, we used to simply split the money up into four different annuity accounts to take advantage of all four investing options. However, the life insurance and annuity industry has addressed the issue of competing investment options and several companies now offer an indexed annuity that allows you to invest in one or more of the four options, usually in whatever percentage you want.

For example, more than a year ago we helped a client and her son, the trustee, with planning for Medicaid using irrevocable trusts. They liked the option of investing her money in an indexed annuity that had the following option and portions chosen:

- Indexed annuity tied to the S&P 500. This investment portion could be calculated annually, monthly over one year periods, every two years, and every three years. They chose monthly over one year periods, and they devoted twenty-five percent (25%) of the money invested into this portion.

- Fixed annuity. This investment portion simply had a fixed rate of interest over a one-year period, and the security of knowing this would pay set interest was attractive enough for them to devote twenty-five percent (25%) to this portion.

- Real estate. Real estate was also attractive as an investment, but there was absolutely no way any of the family members wanted to be involved in the flipping or rental of properties. So they also wanted to commit twenty-five percent (25%) to this portion.

- Gold. Finally, they also discussed the possible ramifications if the market went down, and they wanted to make sure that there was some kind of hedge against a bad market and bad economy, so they also devoted twenty-five percent (25%) to this portion of the annuity.

In all, they wanted to really balance this indexed annuity and "diversify" even the guaranteed safe investments equally among the four different options.

Different clients have different goals and desires even among their guaranteed safe investments, so these kinds of indexed annuities are often appropriate for them. But just because there are four options doesn't mean you have to devote investments equally like these clients did.

We recently started working with a client who loves real estate and made some significant money over the years in the real estate market, but he is not willing to be a landlord or flip properties anymore. So he is planning on devoting fifty percent (50%) to the real estate portion. He also likes the security of a fixed rate of interest on some of his money, so he may put almost a third into that for thirty-three percent (33%) in the fixed portion. He didn't want to put anything in the stock indexes, so we are not looking at using the S&P 500 index at all. But he did like the idea of some money being in gold, so he is looking to devote the remaining seventeen percent (17%) to that portion.

And the good news is that he can change these allocations, more or less, on an annual basis. But there are some restrictions on these changes because of the particular real estate investment portion he was looking at since it is based on three years of performance. For him, though, he is certain about the real estate portion, and he might want to realign the gold or fixed portions next year, which would be perfectly fine with the annuity he has chosen.

As you can see, there are many varied types of annuities, and there are very specific options that come along with them. But understanding the basics of annuities can help you look more closely at specific options if annuities fit into your overall investment strategy.

Chapter Ten: Life Insurance

"What do you mean, use life insurance as part of my retirement plan?" Patsy asked skeptically. "Life insurance is for when you're dead. Isn't it? How does life insurance benefit me?"

It really is a different concept, but one that can provide some major advantages to our clients depending on how they want to use it. However, it's sometimes difficult to explain just because of the indoctrination surrounding what is quickly becoming known as "the old type of life insurance." It's not just about a death benefit payout to beneficiaries anymore.

"It's going to sound unfamiliar, but it really can dramatically help with your retirement if the situation is right," I said. "You can actually put money into a certain kind of life insurance policy in a lump sum for a specific death benefit, and then just borrow against the death benefit when you need money. You are not borrowing against your cash value, though. You are actually borrowing against the death benefit for these types of policies."

"But why would I want to take out a loan?" Patsy said. "It's my money, isn't it? And I'm assuming I'd have to pay interest on the loan and make payments."

"Actually, no, you wouldn't have to make payments, nor would you ever have to pay the loan back yourself," I said. "The insurance company just charges a relatively low rate of interest on what you borrowed, and then the loan is paid back from the life insurance proceeds after you die."

"So I would be paying interest, even if it is at my death, wouldn't I?" she asked.

"Yes, but let me ask a question," I said. "What will be your income tax rate during retirement?"

"Probably the 25% tax bracket," Patsy said. "What does that have to do with anything?"

"Well, which would you rather do," I started to ask. "Put your money in an IRA and have to pay 25% in taxes whenever you took money out, or would you rather have your heirs pay the loan and accumulated interest, and at likely less than 5% interest, out of the death benefit?"

"Well, that sounds like a no-brainer," Patsy said.

"I agree," I replied. "There are always items of fine print to consider, and we always need to run the numbers, but at least I think this something we should look into."

"OK," Patsy said. "What do we need to do first?"

Life insurance is not a one-size fits all proposition anymore, and there are many, many permutations available. But the basic concepts of life insurance are still the same:

- You pay money to a life insurance company;
- There is a contract detailing all of the rights, responsibilities, and benefits; and
- When you die, there is a death benefit paid out to chosen beneficiaries.

The details around all of those points are extremely varied. As legislation and regulation grew around life insurance, the loopholes that people can take advantage of also grew. The insurance companies responded each step of the way by coming up with more creative options that, depending on a person's particular needs and goals, could do far more than just pay a death benefit to beneficiaries. That is where a great distinction is now being made by financial advisors around "the old life insurance" versus "the new life insurance."

There is not enough time and pages to go into all of the different features, and you wouldn't want to read through them all anyway. By far, the best answer is to see what interests you and may apply, and then speak to someone who has access to a lot of different life insurance options and get numbers. We work with people all of the time to see what can be done to creatively help solve their problems and reach their goals.

But first, let's take a quick look at the main types of life insurance and then look at a hypothetical example of borrowing against a death benefit for retirement planning purposes.

Term Life Insurance

This is the type of life insurance that most people under 50 are used to hearing about. Term life insurance pays a death benefit to your chosen beneficiaries if you die during the life of the policy, and you pay regularly for the coverage for an established length of time. The terms can be any number of years, but usually you see them in increments of 5 years and usually up to 20 years, although there are some out there for a greater length of time.

For example, if you purchased a 20 year term policy for $1 million at age 30, it will cover you until age 50 provided you kept paying the premiums. If you passed on at age 45, the $1 million goes to the person or people you named as your beneficiaries. If you don't pass on by the end of the 20 years, then the policy goes away. As I said, there always options, and one of those options, depending on the policy, the ability to renew the life insurance policy for an established or varied new premium amount, but in some cases the policy just ends and you need to get a new life insurance policy if you want it.

One type of term policy that we should specifically mention is what is called "group life insurance," meaning the life insurance you get through work. This may be available as part of employment, and the payout amount may be a set dollar figure or some factor of your annual salary, such as "two times your annual salary." In many cases, the life insurance "term" is for as long as you stay employed with the company, but some states mandate that you be allowed to "take the life insurance with you" if you leave employment, but then the premiums are your responsibility, and there may be a length of time imposed on the policy. The one distinguishing benefit of taking the insurance with you is that you often don't have to prove "insurability."

Unfortunately, as part of my legal estate planning practice, we sometimes have to deal with a situation where someone younger is dying and they reach a point when they can no longer work. Part of our planning is making sure that we examine their group life insurance and look at options to continue it if it will still be cost effective to do so even though the premiums are now being paid directly instead of through the employer.

Permanent

I often have life insurance agents look at me a little funny when I describe a category of insurance as "permanent" instead of by one of the industry terms they are used to hearing, such as universal life, whole life, or some other variation. Part of what makes me The Plain English Attorney™ is that I try to keep it simple. The fact that the life insurance policy has no set term is what makes it permanent. Whether the policy needs you to keep paying periodically, or you can pay a lump sum, or you can pay a lump sum and add more later, the distinguishing feature is that it doesn't go away in a set number of years.

Now I do have put a caveat here. Some permanent life insurance policies do have an expiration *age*, but not a set number of years. That usually means that at that age the policy just pays the death benefit to the owner of the policy. In other words, if the policy has an expiration age of 110 and the insured lives to 110, then the company will pay the death benefit to the owner or someone else specified in the policy. I usually joke with my clients and tell them if they reach that age, then the company acknowledges that they "win."

Borrowing Against Life Insurance Example

Patsy's situation is not unique, but it is also is not as common as some other financial situations. If you have a decent amount of non-deferred investments, meaning you have already paid the income taxes on that investment money, and you don't immediately need that money for living or other expenses, then this is a strategy that can work to your advantage. The key benefits are:

- There are no income taxes immediately due and payable when you take money out since it is a loan you are taking out. This does not mean that there will not ever be taxes due, but instead it means that any taxes can be deferred until the death benefit pays out after you are gone. The taxes and the loan can be paid back out of the life insurance proceeds rather than you handling it on an annual basis.

- The loan rates may be significantly less than income tax rates on money put into tax-deferred retirement accounts and later withdrawn.

- If you put more money into tax deferred retirement accounts versus the life insurance policy, then you might just be giving your heirs a tax bomb if it isn't handled correctly, so the life insurance can end up being an income tax break over two generations.

So let's take a look at a couple, both 50 years old, and both planning to work until age 65. They have the ability to put away $500,000 over the next 15 years, and they need to decide whether to put more money into tax deferred accounts or put it into a life insurance policy. Upon retiring, they'll each have $75,000 a year in retirement and social security, meaning they'll have $150,000 a year coming in as a couple, but they want another $40,000 a year in retirement.

They also want to be safe and secure in their investments, so if they use a retirement account, they'll want it to be a fixed rate of interest, and the best they can find is 5% per year. For purposes of these examples, we'll say they both live to 85 years of age.

Here's what investing in an IRA at 5% a year looks like (technically, this is combing two IRAs into one data set, but the total of the numbers still work):

Year	Deposit	Growth	Total retirement Income with pensions, etc.	Withdrawals	Balance	Taxes paid on account withdrawals
1	$33,333.33	5%			$ 35,000.00	
2	$33,333.33	5%			$ 69,999.99	
3	$33,333.33	5%			$ 104,999.99	
4	$33,333.33	5%			$ 139,999.99	
5	$33,333.33	5%			$ 174,999.98	
6	$33,333.33	5%			$ 209,999.98	
7	$33,333.33	5%			$ 244,999.98	
8	$33,333.33	5%			$ 279,999.97	
9	$33,333.33	5%			$ 314,999.97	
10	$33,333.33	5%			$ 349,999.97	
11	$33,333.33	5%			$ 384,999.96	
12	$33,333.33	5%			$ 419,999.96	
13	$33,333.33	5%			$ 454,999.95	
14	$33,333.33	5%			$ 489,999.95	
15	$33,333.33	5%			$ 524,999.95	
16	$0.00	5%	$150,000	$ 40,000.00	$ 511,249.94	$ 11,200.00
17	$0.00	5%	$150,000	$ 40,000.00	$ 496,812.44	$ 11,200.00
18	$0.00	5%	$150,000	$ 40,000.00	$ 481,653.06	$ 11,200.00
19	$0.00	5%	$150,000	$	$	$

				40,000.00	465,735.72	11,200.00
20	$0.00	5%	$150,000	$ 40,000.00	$ 449,022.50	$ 11,200.00
21	$0.00	5%	$150,000	$ 40,000.00	$ 431,473.63	$ 11,200.00
22	$0.00	5%	$150,000	$ 40,000.00	$ 413,047.31	$ 11,200.00
23	$0.00	5%	$150,000	$ 40,000.00	$ 393,699.68	$ 11,200.00
24	$0.00	5%	$150,000	$ 40,000.00	$ 373,384.66	$ 11,200.00
25	$0.00	5%	$150,000	$ 40,000.00	$ 352,053.89	$ 11,200.00
26	$0.00	5%	$150,000	$ 40,000.00	$ 329,656.59	$ 11,200.00
27	$0.00	5%	$150,000	$ 40,000.00	$ 306,139.42	$ 11,200.00
28	$0.00	5%	$150,000	$ 40,000.00	$ 281,446.39	$ 11,200.00
29	$0.00	5%	$150,000	$ 40,000.00	$ 255,518.71	$ 11,200.00
30	$0.00	5%	$150,000	$ 40,000.00	$ 228,294.64	$ 11,200.00
31	$0.00	5%	$150,000	$ 40,000.00	$ 199,709.37	$ 11,200.00
32	$0.00	5%	$150,000	$ 40,000.00	$ 169,694.84	$ 11,200.00
33	$0.00	5%	$150,000	$ 40,000.00	$ 138,179.58	$ 11,200.00
34	$0.00	5%	$150,000	$ 40,000.00	$ 105,088.56	$ 11,200.00
35	$0.00	5%	$150,000	$ 40,000.00	$ 70,342.99	$ 11,200.00
36	$0.00	5%	$150,000	$ 40,000.00	$ 33,860.14	$ 11,200.00
Totals				$ 840,000.00		$ 235,200.00

Over the course of the couples' lives, they took out $840,000 from the IRAs, but they paid $235,000 of it in taxes at the 28% rate. They also have $33,860.14 of the account left to pay to their beneficiaries.

But let's take a look at the life insurance example. If the same couple instead put $33,333.33 a year into a life insurance policy over fifteen years, and ended up with a death benefit of $1,800,000 to borrow against at 3.5% interest, then here is what they would have:

Year	Deposit	Growth	Total retirement Income with pensions, etc.	Borrow amount	Cash Balance	Loan interest rate	Loan Balance	Death benefit
1	$33,333.33	5%			$ 35,000.00	3.50%		
2	$33,333.33	5%			$ 69,999.99	3.50%		
3	$33,333.33	5%			$ 104,999.99	3.50%		
4	$33,333.33	5%			$ 139,999.99	3.50%		
5	$33,333.33	5%			$ 174,999.98	3.50%		
6	$33,333.33	5%			$ 209,999.98	3.50%		
7	$33,333.33	5%			$ 244,999.98	3.50%		
8	$33,333.33	5%			$ 279,999.97	3.50%		
9	$33,333.33	5%			$ 314,999.97	3.50%		
10	$33,333.33	5%			$ 349,999.97	3.50%		
11	$33,333.33	5%			$ 384,999.96	3.50%		
12	$33,333.33	5%			$ 419,999.96	3.50%		
13	$33,333.33	5%			$ 454,999.95	3.50%		
14	$33,333.33	5%			$ 489,999.95	3.50%		
15	$33,333.33	5%			$ 524,999.95	3.50%		$ 1,800,000.00
16	$0.00	5%	$150,000	$ 40,000.00	$ 551,249.94	3.50%	$ 40,000.00	$ 1,760,000.00
17	$0.00	5%	$150,000	$ 40,000.00	$ 578,812.44	3.50%	$ 81,400.00	$ 1,718,600.00
18	$0.00	5%	$150,000	$	$	3.50%		$

				40,000.00	607,753.06		$122,800.00	1,677,200.00
19	$0.00	5%	$150,000	$ 40,000.00	$ 638,140.72	3.50%	$164,200.00	$ 1,635,800.00
20	$0.00	5%	$150,000	$ 40,000.00	$ 670,047.75	3.50%	$205,600.00	$ 1,594,400.00
21	$0.00	5%	$150,000	$ 40,000.00	$ 703,550.14	3.50%	$247,000.00	$ 1,553,000.00
22	$0.00	5%	$150,000	$ 40,000.00	$ 738,727.65	3.50%	$288,400.00	$ 1,511,600.00
23	$0.00	5%	$150,000	$ 40,000.00	$ 775,664.03	3.50%	$329,800.00	$ 1,470,200.00
24	$0.00	5%	$150,000	$ 40,000.00	$ 814,447.23	3.50%	$371,200.00	$ 1,428,800.00
25	$0.00	5%	$150,000	$ 40,000.00	$ 855,169.59	3.50%	$412,600.00	$ 1,387,400.00
26	$0.00	5%	$150,000	$ 40,000.00	$ 897,928.07	3.50%	$454,000.00	$ 1,346,000.00
27	$0.00	5%	$150,000	$ 40,000.00	$ 942,824.48	3.50%	$495,400.00	$ 1,304,600.00
28	$0.00	5%	$150,000	$ 40,000.00	$ 989,965.70	3.50%	$536,800.00	$ 1,263,200.00
29	$0.00	5%	$150,000	$ 40,000.00	$ 1,039,463.99	3.50%	$578,200.00	$ 1,221,800.00
30	$0.00	5%	$150,000	$ 40,000.00	$ 1,091,437.19	3.50%	$619,600.00	$ 1,180,400.00
31	$0.00	5%	$150,000	$ 40,000.00	$ 1,146,009.04	3.50%	$661,000.00	$ 1,139,000.00
32	$0.00	5%	$150,000	$ 40,000.00	$ 1,203,309.50	3.50%	$702,400.00	$ 1,097,600.00
33	$0.00	5%	$150,000	$ 40,000.00	$ 1,263,474.97	3.50%	$743,800.00	$ 1,056,200.00
34	$0.00	5%	$150,000	$ 40,000.00	$ 1,326,648.72	3.50%	$785,200.00	$ 1,014,800.00
35	$0.00	5%	$150,000	$ 40,000.00	$ 1,392,981.16	3.50%	$826,600.00	$ 973,400.00
36	$0.00	5%	$150,000	$ 40,000.00	$ 1,462,630.21	3.50%	$868,000.00	$ 932,000.00
Totals				**$ 840,000.00**			**$ 28,000.00**	**$ 932,000.00**

In this example, the couple withdrew the same $840,000, but they didn't have to pay any taxes on it, just 3.5% interest on the loan. The total interest on the loan at the time of death was $28,000. AND they still had $932,000 to leave to their heirs. By using this strategy, the heirs netted $898,139.86 over the IRA strategy.

But what about tax deductions for the IRA? Assuming no other deductions and the $150,000 per year combined salary, putting away the $33,333.33 each year would save $9,333.33 in taxes for 15 years for a total savings of $139,999.95. Even if you add that back at the end (which assumes the couple didn't just spend their tax savings, which is typical), the life insurance strategy still netted the family $758,139.91 AND they actually were able to spend the full extra $40,000 a year in retirement instead of only $28,800 per year because of the taxes that had to come out.

While there are lots of other ramifications and every situation is different, especially when it comes to taxes, using a strategy of borrowing against a life insurance death benefit is not something people should ignore. Of course, the only way to really know if it will work for you is to get real numbers for this type of life insurance for your specific situation.

Chapter Eleven: Long Term Care

Gus and Wilma were very nervous about long term care costs. After all, Wilma's mother had dementia, as did Wilma's grandmother. Unfortunately, neither of them had long term care insurance, and they both ended up spending every last penny on their care, leaving the family with nothing. And while Wilma knew I was a Certified Medicaid Planner™, her brother was the one in charge, and he didn't want to listen to anyone.

But now that Wilma's mother had passed on, she wanted to know what could be done so her children didn't lose everything if she or her husband Gus had to go to the nursing home.

"But long term care is so expensive!" Wilma said. "We can never afford it! Plus if we never use it, we're just pouring money down the drain."

"But which type of long term care solution are you talking about?" I asked.

Blank stares came back at me.

"What do you mean?" her husband asked me. "Long term care insurance is long term care insurance. It's all the same. Isn't it?"

I smiled, because it definitely wasn't. Not anymore. But now they had a lot of options.

"No, it is definitely not one-size fits all anymore," I said. "There are a lot of different ways we can address potential long term care costs, and traditional long term care insurance is only one way to do it. And in a lot of cases, you're right. It might be just pouring money down the drain. But then again, it might not be. Let's take a look at your options…"

No discussion about financial planning would really be complete without mentioning long term care costs and some different ways to address it, financially or otherwise. But the usual solution of long term care insurance is often the least effective and most costly by the time people think to purchase it. However, long term care insurance is only one of several main solutions that should be looked at, if for no other reason than making sure that all of the hard work you put into building your finances isn't wiped out, leaving nothing for your family.

One of the reasons that long term care insurance is so expensive and is often bypassed as unaffordable is that it wasn't always so. Go back 20 or 30 years, and companies were selling long term care insurance like crazy, and, while still pricey, it was generally affordable. So what happened? Why didn't the premiums just rise with inflation like everything else?

Well, all things being equal that's exactly what should have happened. But it wasn't "equal." When you go back those 20-30 years, the average nursing home stay was somewhere around 7 months when the patient either left the facility or passed on. When the insurance companies created the long term care policies, they based the annual premiums on those figures. The companies also frequently put in certain price guarantees that the rates wouldn't rise too steeply.

Flash forward those same 20-30 years, and now the average nursing home stay is closer to 29 months. That's because medicine has advanced so much that it can make people physically healthy for longer periods of time, but there have been no breakout cures for seniors who need 24 hour supervision, particularly in the areas of Alzheimer's or dementia. Now the companies are losing money on long term insurance, and they can't sustain it. Because the companies are often involved in much more than just long term care insurance, they can't afford to not pay out on the policies they sold because it would crush their other business. (Plus keeping your contractual word is just the right thing to do.) So they will honor those agreements, but they will charge much, much more for new policies. That's provided the company still wishes to remain in the long term care market… many are dropping out and just not selling new policies.

So what is still out there?

Traditional Long Term Care Insurance

Even though it has grown much more expensive in recent years, traditional long term care insurance is still worth a discussion. Without taking a look at your specific age and health situation, you might not see that long term care insurance just might be affordable *for you* after all. Each year you delay, it becomes more and more expensive. And with each year that passes by in general, long term care itself is becoming more expensive and rates go up accordingly. Therefore, we often tell our clients not to wait too long to see if traditional long term care insurance might work for them, because there's no telling whether or not it will be out of reach in five or ten years.

Annuities with Long Term Care Provisions

Without going too much into different types of annuities again, often the same or similar types of investments for annuities can be looked at but with different long term care provisions in mind. Generally, there are two main specific strategies to look at.

The first are annuities that have "riders" attached to them that will provide for specific long term care withdrawals benefits without penalties or surrender charges. Many annuities will promise and deliver on certain growth milestones, but you have to agree to leave the money invested for a period of time. For example, a common annuity might be for ten years, and there is an allowed ten percent (10%) withdrawal each year without penalties or surrender charges. But if you need more than that 10%, then the company will often impose fees and surrender charges. However, with the favorable long term care provisions you are paying a little bit extra for (or not, depending on the annuity contract and company), these fees and charges are waived if the money is needed for long term care. The reason the annuity company can afford to provide some long term care coverage in these situations is because they can make the numbers work when they have the annuity money plus the added cost of the insurance being paid on a regular basis, or if not paid for it has been factored in by the company. And the good part is that if you don't need to tap into the money for long term care costs, then it still is just an investment annuity.

The second strategy is a specific type of long term care annuity that will provide a factor of your initial deposit if you need long term care. For example, if you put $300,000 into this specific type of annuity, it will have the usual investment options. Let's say over the course of five years, it grows to $370,000, and at that point you need long term care. The annuity may have specifically provided that you could withdraw up to 2 times your deposit for long term care needs, meaning up to $600,000 is available for long term care needs even though the annuity value is otherwise only at $370,000. The downside is that these annuities sometimes have lower growth than other annuities, but the purpose for the money being put into the annuity is usually security of the principal and to be there for long term care. And when compared to actually paying for traditional long term care insurance, you and your family may come out way ahead.

Permanent Insurance with Borrowing

In the last chapter, we specifically looked at permanent insurance being paid into a life insurance policy then money can be borrowed against the death benefit as a way to tax-effectively plan for retirement. Basically, you borrow money that is not paid back until you are gone and it is just taken out from the death benefit proceeds before going to the beneficiaries.

There are some permanent life insurance policies that may be specifically designed to help cover the costs of long term care rather than retirement. The terms are just a little different. For example, the general borrowing rate might be higher. In the previous chapter we used 3.5% as a borrowing rate, but this type of policy might be more like 4.5%. However, and this is the big factor, borrowing may be at only 2% if the money borrowed is to pay for long term care costs. So the numbers will work out very differently if the intent is to use permanent life insurance for retirement versus for paying for long term care costs. You might be trading off a bigger death benefit for more favorable terms in borrowing money out for long term care purposes, but that might be exactly what you need if the purpose is to potentially use the money for long term care.

The Long Term Care Solution with Trusts

Another, possible strategy for dealing with long term care costs isn't really financial at all. In fact, it involves divesting your assets and control over them, and it's a strategy that many families are turning to, and that is qualifying for Medicaid. I won't go too deeply into this subject in this book because I have another entire book on this called *The Long Term Care Solution*. I also have yet another book on the subject of qualifying for a veteran's pension benefit called *The Veteran's Long Term Care Solution* that lets a veteran, their spouse, or their surviving spouse qualify for the pension and at the same time position their assets for eventual Medicaid qualification. But we will cover just the basics of Medicaid qualification here.

In the United States, there is a specific Medicaid program designed to help seniors pay for long term care costs, provided they meet certain financial restrictions and guidelines (in addition to the health guidelines). At the time of this book being written, a senior must have less than $2,000, is allowed to own a home of less than about $525,000 in equity, a vehicle, and their personal possessions. If they do qualify and receive assistance for Medicaid, then their home will have a lien placed against it for the amount Medicaid spent, but this is not claimed by Medicaid until the person passes on. In addition, all income (with a few exceptions) goes to the nursing home first, and the Medicaid will pick up the difference. Some states also have a limit on the amount of income a person can have, but that is easily bypassed. (Again, see The Long Term Care Solution.)

The biggest restriction is that a person applying for Medicaid cannot have gifts or transfers within the last five years prior to submitting their application. So here's where the trusts come in. Typically, we set up two irrevocable trusts; one for real estate, and one for everything else, and there are some tax reasons for them being a bit different. Now most of the assets are transferred into these trusts in order to get the "five year clock" going for Medicaid, so that five years and one month after transferring the assets, Medicaid no longer "sees" or counts the transfers.

There are two big items that I need to mention:

- The client cannot be in charge of the trusts, nor be the beneficiary of the trusts. They are essentially handing over all of those assets to the trustee (usually an adult child or trusted friend or family member) and trusting that they'll use the money for their benefit. Because of these restrictions, not too many of my clients want to utilize this option until they see a genuine problem down the road.

- Just directly giving the assets to a child or the children can sometimes lead to BIG problems down the road. If a child passes on before you do, and their spouse inherits all of the money you gave them, will that surviving spouse still use the money for your benefit? What if the one child holding all of your assets is sued, and your money is claimed in the lawsuit? If you gave the assets to all of your children, what happens if one of them ends up in some financial difficulty and can't pitch in "their fair share" of certain costs, and now there are problems among the children? There are just too many variables and contingencies that can come up that we frequently suggest using the irrevocable trusts over direct gifts.

As I mentioned, there is a lot more information in my two books, but I at least wanted to make sure that we covered the basics of long term care planning. After all, potential long term care costs can cause your entire financial plan to explode to the tune of $7,000 to $12,000 or more each month for nursing level care.

Chapter Twelve:
A Financial Planning Process

Many years before I started helping my clients on the financial end of planning, it seemed that every new financial advisor and life insurance agent was calling my law office. They all wanted to "send me clients," to get their foot in the door, but what they really wanted was to work with my clients. However, the vast majority were just selling the "product of the week" to people. No matter what their situation, no matter what stage of life they were in, they always magically had the exact same perfect solution that was appropriate for all of my clients.

That wasn't what we wanted. We wanted to work with professionals who had a definite, broad process for helping their clients with their finances, and we really weren't seeing it in the professionals calling and emailing us. And in most cases, they weren't sending us any of their clients. But the requests to meet with me to discuss the advisors sending me clients still came. If we had the time, we were still meeting with as many as two or three financial advisors a week, and almost all the time it went nowhere. Eventually, I had to put a stop to it.

"Here are the new rules about appointments with financial advisors who want to meet with me to discuss sending me clients," I told my then-office manager.

She frowned at me, reading the guidelines. "Seriously?" she asked.

"Yes," I replied.

"Just so I'm clear, you want me to ask them to explain to me what they do for their clients in less than 30 seconds without using the word 'product" more than once?" my office manager asked. "And if they can't do it, then you don't want to meet with them?"

"That's right," I said.

She started to laugh. "You're going to have a lot fewer meetings," she said.

And that was the point. I don't care what "products" a financial advisor has and can sell. It's not about the products. It's not about the investments. It's not even about rates of return or guarantees. It's about a process of finding out what our clients want to accomplish financially in the same way we help our legal clients figure out what their estate planning wishes are. We can then find what is needed to help them reach their financial goals. And, incidentally, that is why I have started using my own financial process and from there plug in the right professionals to help.

Yes, indeed, we had a lot fewer initial meetings with financial professionals. But now we only meet and work with the right ones.

It is unfortunate that there are many financial advisors fixated on the stock market, and they don't adjust investments based on age or retirement needs. For them, they are the hammer and every investment looks like a nail. There are also those financial advisors who are only recommending annuities and life insurance without thought to age or station in life. For them, they are a screwdriver and every product looks like a screw. We have a more systematic approach to discovering which tools are needed for your particular situation and stage of life, *whether or not we personally provide all of those tools*. And we have a process to help uncover that for you.

Over the years, I have seen other financial professionals utilize different methods. Some use a first meeting to "get to know you" without saying hardly anything at all. They have a lot of time to waste, but at the same time people will do business with people they like. That may be fine if there is a specific process. Sometimes there isn't and it is "free flowing." Unfortunately, free flowing can often mean directionless until they stumble upon an investment or product that resonates with you, whether it meets your particular goals or not. Most of my client are more comfortable with a specific process with a defined beginning and end, even if the "end" means we're done with changes and we now move into a monitoring and review mode on a periodic basis.

Other financial advisors who primarily handle stocks will only look at investment risk tolerance alone and then come up with a mix of stocks and bonds to fit the risk tolerance. Usually conservative, moderate, or aggressive. While a little better than just a free flowing, "throw stuff against the wall and see what sticks" series of meetings, it still leaves a lot to be desired. It also, unfortunately, usually just focuses on stocks and bonds as solutions without taking a look at guaranteed secure components such as life insurance and annuities.

We take a different, systematic approach to first analyze what percentage of your assets should be guaranteed safe and what can be at risk, and then look at what the risky portion should be in, meaning conservative, moderate, or aggressive. It is entirely possible that a client of ours may want to keep 75% guaranteed safe, but then have 25% in aggressive stocks. On the other hand, a client of ours may want half guaranteed safe and the other half in conservative, but not guaranteed safe, market securities. But just stopping at conservative, moderate, or aggressive portfolio management is not something we consider a complete enough picture of your financial goals.

Here's our general process:

Pre-Appointment Packet: We mail a packet to our clients with a questionnaire, general office information and policies, a map with directions to our offices, and a copy of this book to read. In order to meet with us, we do require that the packet be reviewed, the book returned, and the questionnaire turned in to our office. We do this because we want to make sure that we are spending our time with people who are up on the basics and are serious enough about their financial plans to take the time to fill out the questionnaire. (Believe it or not, there are a substantial number of people who enjoy meeting and spending time with professionals when they have no intention of doing anything differently. We need to make sure that people who are genuinely trying to better their financial future are taking up the limited number of appointment slots that we have available.)

Financial Strategy Session. The first meeting is called the "Financial Strategy Session," and it lives up to its name. During this meeting, we will go through a series of discussions based on different factors of risk and the tolerance for each, the acceptable level of risk for assets not guaranteed safe, preferences for different kinds of investments both guaranteed safe and at risk, and a few other big "life" factors that need to be considered. At this time, if our clients want us to move forward, we can work on and create a plan summary and some very general recommendations that will be discussed and refined at the next meeting.

Plan Summary Meeting. During the second meeting, we discuss the overall asset and investment plan in broad terms, such as percentages to be placed into stocks or bonds and the corresponding risk levels and/or percentages to be placed in guaranteed safe annuities with particular accumulation options. However, at this stage we are not making specific stock recommendations or going over specific annuities or life insurance from specific companies. We just want to make sure that we have correctly allocated things and discuss any changes our clients might want to make.

Just as an aside, I do not give advice on stocks or bonds, nor do I oversee any kind of market investments. Once we determine what our clients want to have in the stock market, we can recommend a broker who will specifically coordinate with our overall plan, but they will work with our clients to determine any specific mutual funds or brokerage account stocks. I learned a long time ago that our clients need to have the right tool for the right job, and because of the highly regulated nature of the stock industry, I wouldn't be able to write the books that I do in plain English without huge amounts of caveats, disclaimers, and months and months of regulatory review of my writings. It is for this reason that I'm licensed as an attorney and I am licensed to work with life insurance and annuities, and that's enough.

Specific Recommendations Meeting. Once the Plan Summary Meeting is complete, we can now start to make some specific recommendations about what is most appropriate for our clients. For example, the clients may have set goals of 75% of their money to be secure and 25% to be in moderate stocks. They like for some of their secure money to be tied to the S&P 500 index but they also want some of their secure money to be tied to the gold market in case there is a downturn. They also want to make sure that there is a fund for long term care needs at the same time. Then we *may* recommend something like the following:

- First set aside a sufficient fund of assets to handle some unexpected expenses which will be in a money market fund.

- 50% of the remaining investable assets will be placed in ABC Annuity, a hybrid indexed annuity with 2/3 tied to the S&P 500 and the remaining 1/3 tied to a gold fund with very good growth potential;

- 25% of the remaining investable assets placed in XYZ Annuity, which is also a hybrid indexed annuity with 2/3 tied to the S&P 500 and the remaining 1/3 tied to a gold fund with fair to good growth but with great options for long term care funding;

- 25% of the remaining investable assets we would refer to our preferred stock investment professional for placement in moderate mutual funds, bonds, and/or brokerage account stocks depending on the advice of the broker.

Again, this is just a possible scenario, and we would possibly have a few meetings to discuss different options depending on the wishes of our clients.

Financial Paperwork Signing Meeting. Simply, this is when any financial paperwork is signed to reapportion your investable assets in accordance with your goals and the financial plan. For example, if some of your money is being moved from stocks to an annuity, there is often paperwork for both the existing stock company AND the annuity company. We try to get as much of the paperwork as possible handled in this one meeting. However, there are sometimes a few meetings to adjust and correct paperwork, and it has been our experience that financial companies being instructed to release funds to be reinvested elsewhere can be difficult to work with and may use a variety of tactics to hold on to the funds a bit longer. One "unofficial" advantage our clients enjoy in these situations is that in addition to helping with financial matters, I am also an attorney, and a call from me or my law office staff may help move things along.

Financial Funding Meeting. Now that paperwork is signed, any official paperwork from the company or companies that has been sent to us is provided to our clients, and we now also provide an overview of all of their assets in terms of ownership titling, pay-on-death beneficiary designations, and generally making sure that their assets are set up properly to work in coordination with any estate plan they may have in place. After all, it really wouldn't be a good financial plan if the accounts weren't set up to take care of our clients' loved ones should anything happen to them.

Family Review Meeting. Once all of the financial moves have been made, and any account retitling and beneficiary designation changes have been made, then we offer an open meeting to discuss the financial plan with any family members or trusted individuals our clients wish. Sometimes our clients are very eager to make sure that their adult children are well informed of their finances. However, many of our clients have different family dynamics and they simply "don't talk about money" with their children. We nonetheless offer this meeting as part of our process, but whether or not to proceed and how is at the discretion of our clients.

Annual Review. After all of the financial moves have been made to bring your money in line with your goals and objectives, it is important to review things annually. As life changes, your financial situation and aims may also change. To make sure that everyone is still on the same page, *at least* once a year we review the current status of your investments, see if your tolerance for risk has changed, review changes in life circumstances that may impact your plan, review any changes in the law or taxes, and review other options depending on market changes or new opportunities. Some of our clients wish to meet with us more frequently, and we can certainly do so.

As you can see, we have a well-defined framework for helping bring out your goals and objectives in a systematic fashion rather than just holding a series of meetings to see what appeals to you. Unfortunately, we see many financial advisors who do that by having a "get to know you" meeting that really doesn't accomplish anything other than give the opportunity for the financial advisor to get you to like them and give them some idea of what product to pitch at the second meeting. And then if that doesn't work, they hold a third meeting to pitch something else.

And on and on it goes until the client "buys something" or they stop meeting with the advisor. This is not a very productive process that may lead people to get frustrated at the lack of a cohesive plan, but in the end the financial advisor is playing the odds and coming out ahead. But they don't get to help nearly as many people as they could.

When we hold a first meeting, we want to make sure that we are accomplishing something worthwhile to our clients that can lead to developing a solid financial plan and not just chitchat. There is a defined beginning, middle, and end to the process, at least until there is a review scheduled to make sure the plan is still working. But it isn't an open ended series of meetings to just see "what sticks." In this process, we certainly get to know our clients and they get to know us, but that shouldn't be the sole focus of any meeting. Our clients are usually too busy to come to our office just to "get to know us," and we want to be as respectful of their time.

Conclusion

There is a world of financial opportunity out there. But that also means that there are so many different choices, different levels of risk, and different prospects for returns. It doesn't make it any easier that there are financial professionals who have their particular field of products and investments and then look no further than what they have to offer. But having a good overview of the different investments out there and a systematic approach to uncover your goals can go a long way to finding the right financial plan to protect and grow your future.

For more information on financial planning, please contact us at 919-518-8237, or visit the The Care Assistance Center, LLC on the web at www.CareAssistanceCenter.com. For more information on legal estate planning, please contact us at 919-844-7993 or visit us at www.LivingTrustLawFirm.com.

Made in the USA
Monee, IL
04 November 2026

67375740R00079